Revise for

ADVANCED PE for OCR A2

D0532729

Sarah van Wely
John Ireland
Ian Thomas
Daniel Bonney

www.heinemann.co.uk
✓ Free online support
✓ Useful weblinks
✓ 24 hour online ordering

01865 888058

Heinemann
Inspiring generations

Heinemann is an imprint of Pearson Education Limited,
a company incorporated in England and Wales, having
its registered office at Edinburgh Gate, Harlow, Essex, CM20 2JE.
Registered company number: 872828

Heinemann is a registered trademark of
Pearson Education Limited

© Sarah van Wely, John Ireland, Ian Thomas, Danny Bonney, 2004

First published 2004

09

10 9 8 7

British Library Cataloguing in Publication Data is available
from the British Library on request.

ISBN 978 0 435583 14 9

Typeset by TechType, Abingdon, Oxon

Original illustrations © Pearson Education Limited, 2004

Cover photo: © Empics/Topham

Acknowledgements

Every effort has been made to contact copyright holders of material reproduced in this book.
Any omissions will be rectified in subsequent printings if notice is given to the publishers.

Photographs: Figure 1.11 (p21) Topham; Figure 1.16 (p28) Illustrated London News; Figure
1.17 (p29) Hulton Getty; Figure 1.18 (p30) Corbis; Figure 1.20 (p32) Corbis/Hulton Deutsch;
Figure 1.21 (p33) Topham; Figure 1.22 (p34) courtesy of Sarah van Wely; Figure 2.04 (p51)
Getty/Photodisc; Figure 4.02 (p106) Empics/Topham.

Exam questions in chapters one, four and five reproduced courtesy of OCR.

Printed in China (CTPS/07)

Tel: 01865 888058 www.heinemann.co.uk

Contents

Introduction

This book has been produced specifically for students revising for OCR's A2 Physical Education (PE) specification. It contains information on all the topics that are examined in:

- Unit 2565 Physical Education: historical, comparative, biomechanical and sport psychology options
- Unit 2566 Exercise and sport physiology, and the Synoptic question.

This book follows the same structure as *Advanced PE for OCR: A2* also published by Heinemann and contains the key information that you need to know for your examination.

At the beginning of each unit, chapter and section you will find overview charts with tick boxes, which you can use to help plan your revision as well as checking your progress. If you are not satisfied with your level of knowledge and understanding of a particular topic or chapter, then you can revisit those areas.

The book includes certain features to help you:

Need to know more?
This provides cross-references to *Advanced PE for* OCR: A2 if you need further information on a topic.

Key words
These are emboldened in the text and listed separately. These are the key words and terms that you need to know.

Hot tips
These are designed to give you exam help and advice.

Exam practice

At the end of each chapter, you will find a section of exam-style questions. When you have completed your revision for a chapter, you should answer the questions, which will enable you to test your knowledge and understanding as well as practising your exam technique. When you have completed the questions, check your answers with those provided at the end of the book. Compare your marks with 'How did you do?' which gives advice on your next course of action. In some cases, this may involve giving yourself a pat on the back, or it may involve finding out which areas you did not do well in and doing some more work on them.

Unit 4: Physical Education: historical, comparative, biomechanical and sport psychology options

Unit overview

Chapter 1: Historical studies	☐
Chapter 2: Comparative studies	☐
Chapter 3: Biomechanical analysis of human movement	☐
Chapter 4: Psychology of sport performance	☐

Tick the box when you are satisfied with your level of knowledge and understanding for each chapter.

Chapter 1 **Historical studies**

Chapter overview

1. Popular recreation ☐
2. Nineteenth-century public school developments of athleticism ☐
3. Rational recreation in an urban industrial society ☐
4. The development of drill, physical training and physical education in elementary schools ☐

Section 1: *Popular recreation*

Section overview

1. Introduction ☐
2. The characteristics and cultural factors of popular recreation ☐
3. Bathing ☐
4. Rowing ☐
5. The development of sports festivals ☐
6. Games in popular recreation ☐

Tick the box when you are satisfied with your level of knowledge and understanding for each topic within this section.

NEED TO KNOW MORE?

For further information on popular recreation, see pp. 3–22 in *Advanced PE for OCR: A2*.

HOT TIPS

Make sure that you are clear about the dates of the start and end of the eighteenth, nineteenth and twentieth centuries, and remember that anything before 1800 we can call 'pre-industrial'.

1 Introduction

You have studied four aspects of sports history:

- **Popular recreation** – pre-industrial sports and pastimes mainly associated with the lower class. This term could also refer to the most popular pastimes at the time.
- **Nineteenth-century public schools** – old, established, fee-paying schools dominated by upper- and upper-middle-class boys.
- **Rational recreation** – civilised and organised sports and pastimes of post-industrial Britain.
- **State elementary schools** – schools for junior-aged children, maintained by public spending. State education began in Britain following the Forster Education Act of 1870.

You have also considered case study activities, which you have traced from before to after the **Industrial Revolution** (the transformation of society from a rural agricultural system to an urban factory system), and analysed the impact and influence of the public schools on each activity.

Case studies

HOT TIPS

Examiners like answers to the 'why' questions, so try to put historical fact into societal context whenever you can.

Individual activities	Games
Bathing and swimming	Mob football and Association Football
Rowing	Cricket
Athletics	Real tennis and lawn tennis

Sports history can usefully be analysed with reference to:

- What activity was being pursued? (individual or game?)
- Who was taking part? (class and gender)
- When was it done? (pre- or post-industrial, occasional or regular, fixed or spontaneous in terms of time?)
- Where was it done? (rural or urban?)
- Why was it done? (social, entertainment, wagering?)
- How sophisticated was it? (level of structure, violence, etc.)

HOT TIPS

To be an effective A level sports historian, you must try to combine chronology (the order of dates in which events took place) with causation (the relationship between cause and effect), and continuity with change.

If you do all of this, you will be thinking like an historian!

2 The characteristics and cultural factors of popular recreation

Sports and games reflect the society, time and place in which they exist. Pre-industrial popular recreation, therefore, reflected pre-industrial British

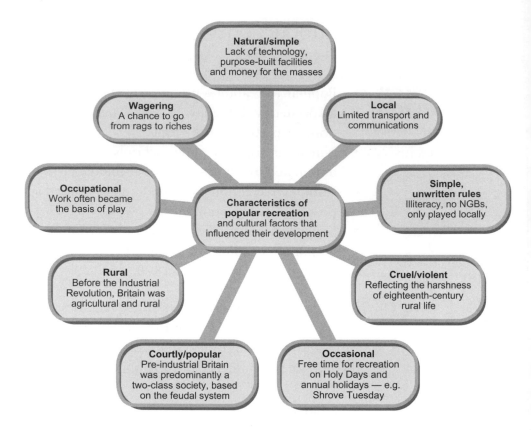

Fig. 1.01 Characteristics of popular recreation.

society. The characteristics of popular recreation are shown in Figure 1.01 above.

Why did popular recreations have these characteristics?

Characteristics of popular recreation	Why?
Local	Limited transport and communications
Simple, unwritten rules	Illiteracy, no NGBs, only played locally
Cruel/violent	Reflecting harsh eighteenth-century rural life
Occasional	Time to play on feast days, Holy Days and annual holidays
Courtly/popular	As a reflection of Britain's predominantly two-class society
Rural	Pre-industrial Britain was mainly agricultural and rural
Occupational	Work sometimes became the basis of play
Wagering	A chance to go from rags to riches
Natural/simple	Lack of alternative places to play

Now, let's revise each of the case study activities as they existed in pre-industrial Britain, that is, as popular recreations.

3 Bathing

What?	Bathing Also on the waterfront: casual informal games, athletics, sports, horse racing, shooting And in winter: sliding, skating, ice fairs	
Who?	Predominantly lower class, but not exclusively	
When?	Hot summer days Occasionally	
Where?	The natural environment The river (and its banks and meadows for other associated activities)	
Why?	Recreation Survival/safety Health/cleanliness Part of the **chivalric code** (the courteous, gallant and gentlemanly behaviour associated with the nobility) Wager races Social gatherings	
How?	From informal 'dips' to the beginnings of competitive swimming and the relatively sophisticated (occasional) ice fairs	

(See p. 16 for swimming and bathing in the public schools.)

4 Rowing

Who?	**Watermen** (men who earned their living on or about boats) Also, locals who might hire boats from local boatmen on summer days	
When?	Occasionally (NB the Doggett Coat and Badge Race for apprentice watermen)	
Where?	Thames, Tees, Tyne, Mersey and any other suitable river	
Why?	Initially functional – for warfare, fishing, travel and commerce Later, recreational Wager races For money (occupational)	
How?	Not cruel or violent, often well organised	

(See p. 17 for rowing in the public schools.)

5 The development of sports festivals

What?	Community activities: rural sports and festivals, commercial fairs and wakes, annual parish feasts and fairs (including grinning contests, whistling matches, etc.)	Pedestrianism and athletics
Who?	Men and women Predominantly lower class (though not exclusively)	Gentry originally employed footmen as messengers. Later, professional athletes were promoted and sponsored by gentry **patrons** (members of the gentry who looked after a lower-class rower, pedestrian or prizefighter. He would arrange the contest, put up stake money, and give board and lodging to the performer. He did it for prestige and because of the contemporary popularity of contests. Today he would be called an agent or sponsor.) Men of all backgrounds were pedestrians. Captain Barclay Allardice attracted a crowd of 10,000 in 1809. Deerfoot (Native American) toured England in 1860s, attracting huge crowds
When?	Annually, occasionally	At height in Regency period (but right up to mid-nineteenth century)
Where?	Rural, village green, etc.	Centred on pubs, between villages, at racecourses
Why?	'Rustic sports' associated with festivity, feasting and fun! Proof of strength and virility for men (e.g. stick fighting, wrestling and running races) Entertainment and prize winning for both sexes	Wager races for money An escape from poverty and hardship Entertainment, social gathering
How?	Generally low levels of organisation Relatively uncouth/ uncivilised (frowned on by the Church)	Initially informal, but at its height pedestrianism was highly structured and organised Head-to-head matches particularly popular Later associated with trickery, corruption, match fixing and some crowd rioting

🔑 KEY WORDS

Patrons

NEED TO KNOW MORE?

For further information on the development of sports festivals, see pp. 14–17 in *Advanced PE for OCR: A2.*

(See p. 17 for athletics in the public schools.)

6 Games in popular recreation

Mob football

What?	Mob football
Who?	Lower class males
When?	Occasionally; often an annual festival, for example Shrove Tuesday or New Year's Day
Where?	Predominantly rural (though some in towns e.g. Kingston-upon-Thames)
Why?	To prove virility, inter-village rivalry, social, drinking, wagering, annual village celebration/feast
How?	Rowdy, violent, locally-coded mauls involving brute force rather than skill, and causing uproar, injury and damage to property

(See p. 17 for football/rugby in the public schools.)

Cricket

What?	Cricket
Who?	Upper and lower class Males and females Some freelance professionals (lower class) – with national touring sides from 1840s
When?	From early eighteenth century Often associated with feasts and festival days A summer game
Where?	Predominantly in rural areas Villages whose cricket sides developed into clubs n.b.: Bat and Ball Inn – Hambledon, Hampshire
Why?	Professionals who played for a living Widespread wagering A social activity bringing classes together
How?	According to rules (first 'Articles of Agreement' written in 1727) By 1774 – more codification 1809 Marylebone Cricket Club (MCC) had standardised rules Rules were adapted locally Predominantly non-violent

(See p. 17 for cricket in the public schools.)

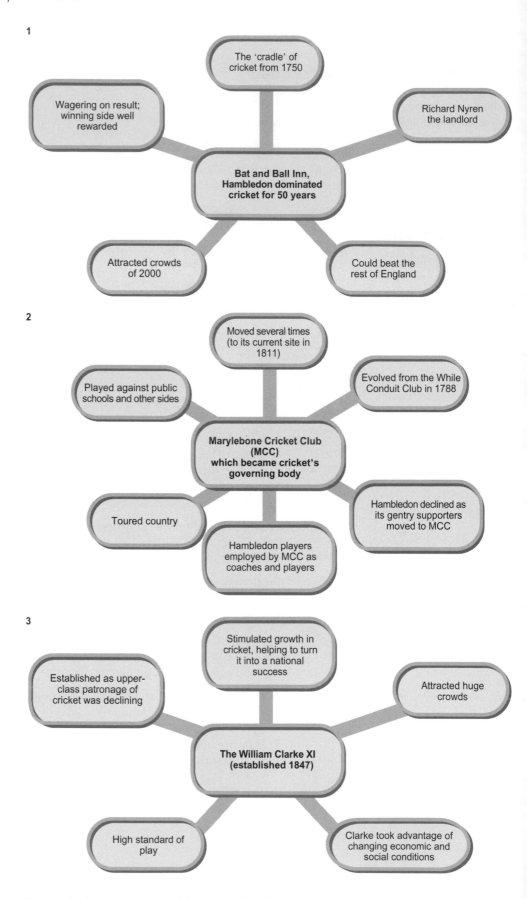

Fig. 1.02 Three key parts of the story of cricket.

Real tennis

HOT TIPS

Be able to compare real tennis with mob football. Think about who played it, where it was played, rule structure, numbers involved, dress, levels of skill or force, regularity of play and so on.

What?	Real tennis
Who?	Exclusively for kings, nobles and merchants Played by Henry VIII (for example at Hampton Court Palace) and by Charles I during **Civil War** between the Royalist Cavaliers (who were gentry, rural and High Church) and the Roundheads (supporters of Parliament and led by Oliver Cromwell, who were merchants, urban and Low Church). Charles I executed in climax of war in 1649. England thus declared a republic, and subsequent harsh puritan lifestyle made it a bleak time for sports and games
When?	Popular in Britain in fourteenth century – throughout Middle Ages and beyond
Where?	Originated in France On purpose-built, highly sophisticated courts
Why?	Recreation, social standing, wagering
How?	With complex rules, specialist equipment and high levels of skill and etiquette

(See p. 17 for tennis and other racquet games in the public schools.)

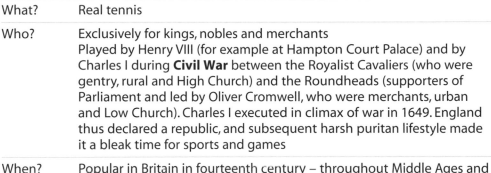 **CHECK !**

Go back to the overview diagrams on p. 2. If you are satisfied with your knowledge and understanding, tick off the sections that you have revised so far. If you are not satisfied, then revisit those sections and refer to the pages in the 'Need to know more?'

Section 2: *Nineteenth-century public school developments of athleticism*

Section overview

1 Introduction ☐

2 Technical and social development ☐

3 Swimming ☐

4 Rowing ☐

5 Athletics ☐

6 Football/rugby ☐

7 Cricket ☐

8 Court and racquet games ☐

NEED TO KNOW MORE?

For further information on public school developments of athleticism, see pp. 22–39 in *Advanced PE for OCR: A2*.

Tick the box when you are satisfied with your level of knowledge and understanding for each topic within this section.

1 Introduction

The focus here is on the emergence of **athleticism** (the combination of physical effort and moral integrity) in nineteenth-century public schools.

Three stages in the development of athleticism will be analysed.

KEY WORDS

Athleticism

Dr Thomas Arnold

Technical developments

Social developments

Values

- Stage one (c. 1790–1824): bullying and brutality.
- Stage two (1828–42): **Dr Thomas Arnold** and social control.
- Stage three (1842–1914): athleticism – the 'cult'.

For each stage you should be aware of:

- **technical developments** – related to rule structure, equipment, facilities, spectatorism, level of skilfulness, etc.
- **social developments** – the influence of social change such as improved transport and communications, as well as changing social relationships within the schools
- **values** – ethics and morals such as teamwork, manliness, loyalty, honour and courage that build 'character' and become guidelines for life.

You must also analyse four extracts from the novel *Tom Brown's Schooldays* by Thomas Hughes (1857). This novel gives considerable insight into life in a public school in the mid-nineteenth century. The extracts are:

- The football match.
- Country pursuits and swimming.
- The fight.
- The cricket match.

You need to be able to identify the characteristics of the major public schools and explain how each characteristic influenced the growth and development of athleticism.

HOT TIPS

An exam question could give you the characteristics and ask you to explain the significance of them, or it could ask you to both identify and explain the characteristics.

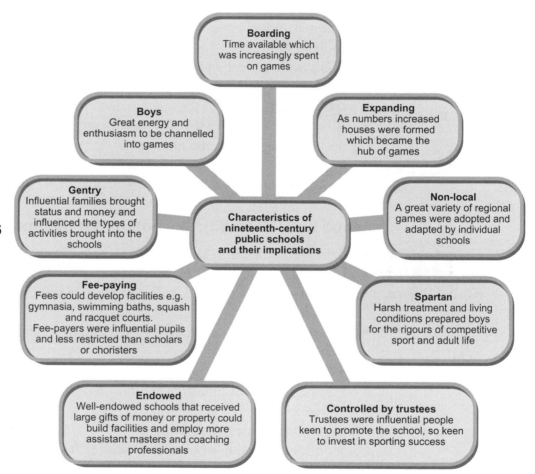

Fig. 1.03 Characteristics of nineteenth-century public schools and their influence on the development of athleticism.

Boarding
Time available which was increasingly spent on games

Boys
Great energy and enthusiasm to be channelled into games

Expanding
As numbers increased houses were formed which became the hub of games

Gentry
Influential families brought status and money and influenced the types of activities brought into the schools

Characteristics of nineteenth-century public schools and their implications

Non-local
A great variety of regional games were adopted and adapted by individual schools

Fee-paying
Fees could develop facilities e.g. gymnasia, swimming baths, squash and racquet courts. Fee-payers were influential pupils and less restricted than scholars or choristers

Spartan
Harsh treatment and living conditions prepared boys for the rigours of competitive sport and adult life

Endowed
Well-endowed schools that received large gifts of money or property could build facilities and employ more assistant masters and coaching professionals

Controlled by trustees
Trustees were influential people keen to promote the school, so keen to invest in sporting success

2 Technical and social development

Stage one (c. 1790–1828): bullying and brutality

- Public school sport, at each stage of development, reflected the broader society in which it existed.
- Sports and pastimes in stage one were a form of 'institutionalised popular recreation'.
- Individual schools were a **melting pot** or mixture of customs and activities from different villages and **preparatory schools** (feeder schools).
- These various games and activities were either adopted (for example, cricket) or adapted (for example, **hare-and-hounds** adapted from hunting, where one boy ran ahead dropping a paper trail as 'scent' for the others to follow).
- Depending on the natural facilities that existed in each school, the adopted and adapted activities from home evolved into each school's sporting culture.
- There were violent games of mob football, bare-knuckle fights and cruelty to animals, alongside childlike games of skipping, hoops and spinning tops.
- All activities were organised by and for the boys themselves with little or no interference from the masters.
- Masters saw their job as stopping at the schoolroom door.
- Discipline could be barbaric and resentment was rife.

KEY WORDS

Melting pot

Preparatory schools

Hare-and-hounds

Stage two (1828–42): Dr Thomas Arnold and social control

- This was a time of reform and **Muscular Christianity** (the combination of godliness and manliness).
- Arnold's main aim, as an ordained clergyman, was to spread the gospel and to produce Christian gentlemen.
- Society was becoming more civilised and as a reflection of that, Dr Arnold was keen to change:
  - the behaviour of boys
  - the severity of punishments imposed by masters
  - the role of the Sixth Form
  - the academic curriculum
  - the relationship of boys and masters from mutual antagonism to mutual trust and respect.
- Arnold wanted to establish **social control** (order, stability and good behaviour). He used games to achieve it.
- He gave the Sixth Form responsibility and increased autonomy in return for their help and support in his mission for change.
- It was through this reform and the development of the **house system** that games increased in status, regularity and organisation.
- The house system became the pivot of public school social and sporting life.

KEY WORDS

Muscular Christianity

Social control

KEY WORDS

House system

Stage three (1842–1914): athleticism – the 'cult'

- By now social control had largely been achieved, both in the public schools and in society at large.
- In this third stage of development games became a **cult** (a craze or obsession) for many boys and even masters.
- Young **assistant masters** taught an academic subject and were fully involved in the games programme, but did not have responsibility for a house.
- Games were now played in their own right and for the values thought to be achievable through them.
- The boys themselves were still predominantly responsible for the organisation of the games programme.
- Professionals were often employed as coaches (e.g. for cricket).
- Personal qualities such as leadership, loyalty, commitment, endeavour and 'pluck' were essential ingredients for any Englishman about to embark on an influential career.
- It was through the careers of such ex-public schoolboys that games and the **games ethic** (a belief that team games could develop character) spread throughout Europe and the **British Empire** (whereby British forms of government, religion, education and culture were also spread to other countries).

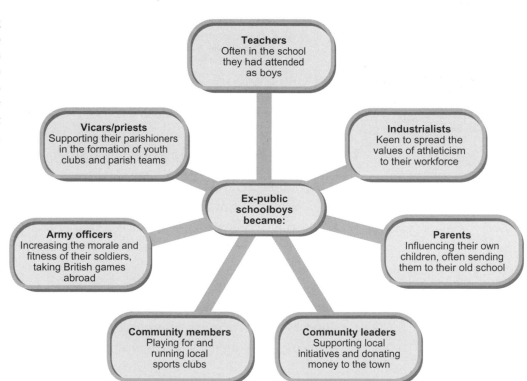

Fig. 1.04 The spread of team games throughout Europe and the British Empire.

Clarendon schools

The **Clarendon schools** were so called because the Earl of Clarendon investigated them (by Royal commission) in 1864. They were the 'big nine' schools of (in date order of foundation): Winchester, Eton, St Paul's, Shrewsbury, Westminster, Merchant Taylor's, Rugby, Harrow and Charterhouse. The Clarendon schools were hugely influential.

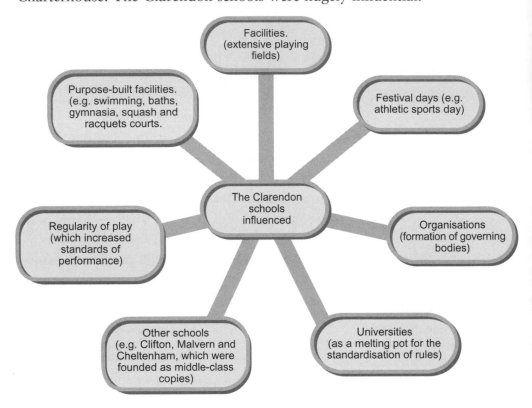

Fig. 1.05 The influence of the Clarendon schools.

The development of athleticism in girls' public and private schools

- Boys'/Public Schools also influenced the development of athleticism in girls' public and private schools.
- Pioneering women such as Frances Buss, Dorothea Beale and Madame Osterberg fought against the tide to encourage physical education and games for girls.
- In spite of their efforts, development for girls lagged behind the boys.
- Over-exertion was thought to be harmful, unladylike, unsuitable and unnecessary. Moreover, appropriate clothing was thought to be far too revealing for young Victorian women.

Tom Brown's Schooldays

The quotations in Figure 1.06 come from the following chapters of the novel *Tom Brown's Schooldays*:

- The football match: part 1, chapter 5.
- Country pursuits and swimming: part 1, chapter 9.
- The fight: part 2, chapter 5.
- The cricket match: part 2, chapter 8.

Read each full extract from a copy of the novel, remembering to look for:

- level and evidence of **technical development**
- different **social relationships** and evidence of social control
- evidence of **values** being identified and/or reinforced as part of the character-building ethic of late nineteenth-century public schools.

The football march

Tom, the new boy, saves the day when he joins in the match between School House and the rest of the school.

Relevant quotations:
'Plush caps have not yet come in, or uniforms of any sort.'
'A safe and well-kept goal is the foundation of all good play.'
Talking of Brooke, the captain, 'wisely and bravely ruling over willing and worshipping subjects, a true football king'.
'This is worth living for; the whole sum of schoolboy existence gathered up into one straining, struggling half hour, a half hour worth a year of common life.'
When Tom joins in, Brooke acknowledges, 'Well, he's a plucky youngster and will make a player.'

Country pursuits and swimming

Tom and his friends go swimming in the river (which was allowed) and also fishing (which was forbidden). They were caught and flogged, and Tom was caught again by the gamekeeper.

Relevant quotations:
Swimming: 'Swift's was reserved for the sixth and fifth forms [the oldest boys], and had a spring board and two sets of steps.'
Fishing (poaching): 'Forgetting landlords, keepers, solemn prohibitions of the Doctor.'
After being taken to the Headmaster, 'Tom was flogged next morning,' and later Tom and the gamekeeper, 'became sworn friends.'

The fight

Tom sticks up for Arthur and fights Slogged Williams.

Relevant quotations:
'There was a strong feeling in the School against catching hold and throwing, though it was generally ruled all fair within limits.'
When Brooke arrives, 'Oh, hurrah! now we shall get fair play.'
When Arnold questions Brooke about not stopping the fight immediately, Brooke explains, 'I thought you wished us to exercise a discretion in the matter too – not to interfere too soon.'
After the fight, 'They're the sort of boys who'll be all the better friends now.'
And Brooke to both boys, 'You must shake hands.'

The cricket match

Tom captains the Rugby School 1st XI in their annual match against MCC.

Relevant quotations:
'It's more than a game. It's an institution.'
'The discipline and reliance on one another which it teaches is so valuable.'
'It merges the individual in the eleven; he doesn't play that he may win, but that his side may.'
'Football and cricket … are such much better games than fives or hare-and-hounds.'
The captain requires, 'skill and gentleness and firmness.'

Fig. 1.06 Summaries of the four extracts from *Tom Brown's Schooldays*.

	Stage one (c. 1790–1828): bullying and brutality	Stage two (1828–42): Dr Thomas Arnold and social control	Stage three (1842–1914): athleticism – the 'cult'
What? (was being played)	From violence of mob football to sedateness of cricket. From casual boating to informal ball games against a wall. 'Institutionalised popular recreation', including poaching and blood sports	A growing programme of games and individual activities as well as boating	A full games and athletics programme according to Governing Body rules especially the major games of cricket and rugby (or Association Football). Also racquets, fives athletics, swimming and rowing in some schools
When? (was it being played)	Free time – outside of lesson time	More regularly often every afternoon	Daily (often compulsory)
Where? (was it being played)	In the school grounds and (where possible) in the surrounding countryside	In the school grounds. Trespass outside curtailed and transport not yet freely available for full programme of inter-school or club matches	Magnificent games fields, purpose-built facilities. On-site and away matches against clubs and schools
Why? (was it being played)	For recreation; to relieve boredom	For social control	For character development
How? (was it being played)	Boys behaving like hooligans. Informally activities ranged from the childlike to the barbaric. Low organisation and structure. As a reflection of popular recreation in society	Boys as Christian gentlemen. Increasingly organised, structured and regulated. On an inter-house basis	As an obsession or cult. Very good standards. Full structure, organisation, kit, equipment and regulations. With sportsmanship and fair play
Swimming	Informal, spontaneous bathing using natural facilities	More regular and regulated bathing (for hygiene, safety and recreation)	For recreation, health, safety and competition. Changing huts, diving boards, purpose-built facilities, galas and attendants

3

		Stage one (c. 1790–1828): bullying and brutality	Stage two (1828–42): Dr Thomas Arnold and social control	Stage three (1842–1914): athleticism – the 'cult'
4	Rowing	Casual boating. Boats hired from local boatyards	More organised rowing (beginning of rowing clubs and master involvement)	Rowing clubs. School boats. **Oxbridge 'blues'** (young men who had represented Oxford or Cambridge in a sporting fixture against the other University) and coaches
5	Athletics	Village 'folk' sports. Hunting, poaching, trespassing, running, exploring the countryside	Restricted and banned (gave school a bad name, annoyed neighbours, against Christian ethics). Hare-and-hounds, steeple chasing	Cross-country running, steeple chasing and cadet corps. School sports days as major sporting and social occasions. NB influence of the Exeter College, Oxford athletics meeting (1850) which was run as a horse race meeting
6	Football/ rugby	Mob games, for example Cloister football at Charterhouse	Football became the place for settling disputes and showing courage and determination. More formalised football rules for individual schools (for example, the running, handling game at Rugby)	Formal rules (FA 1863) 'colours', caps, inter-school fixtures
7	Cricket	Cricket adopted by public schools as non-violent, codified, rural game enjoyed by gentry	Cricket continued (still encouraged due to its non-violent nature, rule structure and upper-class involvement). Inter-house matches	'Colours', caps, regular inter-house and inter-school fixtures, for example versus MCC, professional coaches and assistant masters involved. Often compulsory
8	Court and racquet games	Informal **fives** (a hand-ball game) against any suitable wall. Tennis against suitable walls/buildings NB – not lawn tennis which wasn't invented until the 1870s	Some purpose-built fives courts – still an informal boy culture activity. Racquets developing as more formal alternative	Fives continued as recreational game. Racquets as more formal game of higher status. Also squash. Lawn tennis in girls' schools – low status in boys' schools

Fig. 1.07 Technical developments: the emergence of structured and organised sports and games.

NEED TO KNOW MORE?

For information on the activities in Figure 1.07 as popular recreations, see pp. 17–21 in *Advanced PE for OCR: A2* and pp. 2–9 in this book.

For information on these activities as rational recreations, see pp. 45–53 in *Advanced PE for OCR: A2* and pp. 18–24 in this book.

 CHECK !

Go back to the overview diagrams on p. 2 and 10. If you are satisfied with your knowledge and understanding, tick off the sections that you have revised so far. If you are not satisfied, then revisit those sections and refer to the pages in the 'Need to know more?'

Section 3: *Rational recreation in an urban industrial society*

Section overview

1	Introduction	☐
2	Swimming	☐
3	Rowing	☐
4	Athletics	☐
5	Association Football	☐
6	Cricket	☐
7	Lawn tennis	☐

NEED TO KNOW MORE?

For further information on rational recreation, see pp 39–54 in *Advanced PE for OCR: A2*.

Tick the box when you are satisfied with your level of knowledge and understanding for each topic within this section.

1 Introduction

It is essential that you know the characteristics of rational recreation and understand the cultural or societal factors that influenced their development.

You should also be able to compare the characteristics of rational recreation with those of popular recreation and understand the different societal factors underlying the changes. You could be asked to compare characteristics, societal determinants or activities.

HOT TIPS

A good way to remember some of the characteristics of rational recreation is to think of the letter 'R' – they were rule based, regular, regional, restrictive (class-wise), refined, respectable (with clearly defined) roles – such as goal keeper.

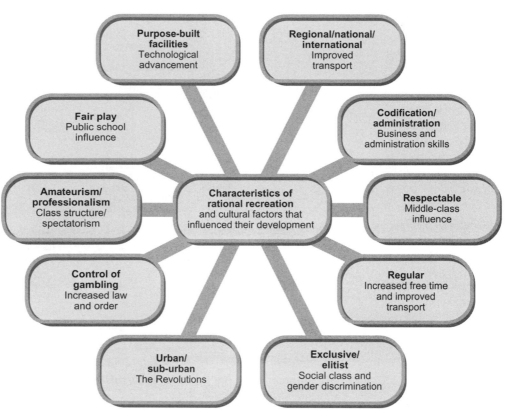

Fig 1.08 The characteristics of rational recreation and cultural factors that influenced them.

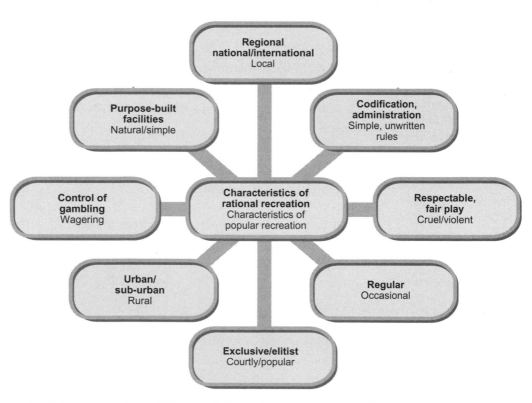

Fig 1.09 Comparison of characteristics: rational recreation and popular recreation.

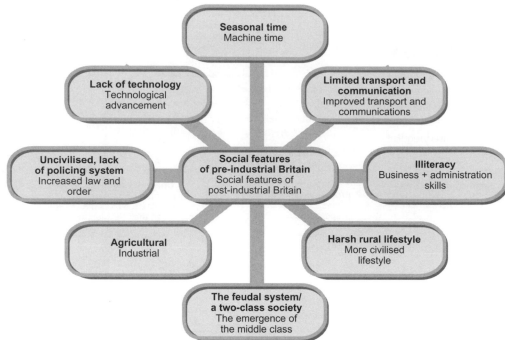

Fig. 1.10 Comparison of pre- and post-industrial societal factors that influenced sport.

Life and times were changing. The Industrial Revolution was, in many ways, also a sporting revolution, with urban industrial factors having a profound effect on the development of sports and games.

• As in pre-industrial times, the class system was rigid and supremely influential in terms of lifestyle and opportunities.
• In post-industrial Britain, however, the emergence of the new middle class must be considered alongside the pre-existing upper and lower classes.
• The new, respectable middle class not only embraced the idea of sports and games, but invented some (for example, lawn tennis) and adapted others (for example, football).

The Industrial Revolution restricted opportunities for the working class to take part in their traditional sports and pastimes. For them, the first half of the nineteenth century was a time of gloom, decay and, in many cases, abject poverty. The popular recreations of the lower classes were curtailed due to lack of:

A **A**cceptance of their traditional activities (due to 'respectable' middle class)
S **S**pace to play (due to urbanisation/over-crowding)
H **H**ealth/energy (due to slaving in the factories)

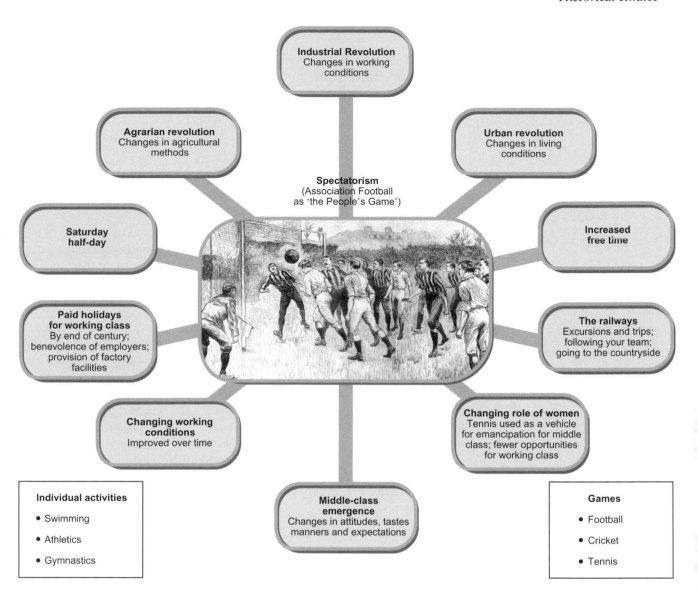

Fig. 1.11 Urban industrial factors influencing the development of rational recreation.

I **Influence** (due to being controlled by their social superiors)

R **Rights** (due to changes in criminal law/police enforcement/RSPCA)

T **Time** (due to 72-hour week /reduction in number of saint's Holy days).

Opportunities improved in the second half of the century, however, as:

- public baths were provided
- industrialists made facilities available to their workers
- factory owners provided excursion trips
- the Church provided opportunities for sports and games through Sunday school and parish teams
- improved transport and communications increased opportunities for spectatorism
- the influence of ex-public schoolboys and their games ethic spread.

Not surprisingly, our case study activities were changing to mirror societal change. In general, as society became more orderly, structured, civilised and well behaved, games and sports did too.

To revise the following activities as popular recreations, pp. 2 to 9, and to revise them in the public schools, see pp. 10 to 18.

HOT TIPS

Outbreaks of cholera spread rapidly through the country, killing thousands and leaving countless families without a breadwinner. The first Public Health Act in 1848 and the building of public baths sought to reduce such problems.

HOT TIPS

Remember public baths:

- prevented the spread of disease
- increased work efficiency
- were used for washing, pleasure and sport.

KEY WORDS

Water cure

Clifton

Exclusion clause

2	Swimming	Rationalised swimming stemmed from:		
		The Regency Spa movement	**Victorian sea bathing**	**Nineteenth-century public baths**
		First, for the upper class in inland spas such as Bath, which became fashionable resorts. By the mid-nineteenth century these resorts were famous for their '**water cure**', a belief in the therapeutic effects of immersion in water. They were subsequently 'invaded' by the emerging middle class, who also often established prestigious schools, for example **Clifton**, (Bristol). Clifton, Malvern and Cheltenham are examples of middle-class copies of Clarendon schools. They took on the games ethic, had outstanding facilities and were each built in spa towns or suburbs. Meanwhile, the gentry moved on to the seaside.	Seaside bathing for the upper class (and the belief in the therapeutic effect of a cold 'dip') was an alternative to a visit to a continental spa. As the restrictive Victorian codes took hold, beaches were socially exclusive and single sexed. By the 1870s, the improved rail network meant that the working class could get to the seaside.	Eighteenth- and nineteenth-century industrialisation and urbanisation initiated the building of urban public baths. Various Acts of Parliament were passed to decrease disease and improve hygiene. In time, swimming clubs for the middle class were established and the Amateur Swimming Association was formed in 1884.
3	Rowing	Amateur regattas such as the University Boat Race and the Henley Regatta reflected the middle-class Victorian craze of combining sport with a good day out. These events stemmed from early river festivals such as the Doggett Coat and Badge Race on the Thames (established 1715). In common with amateur swimmers and athletes, middle-class rowers were determined to keep out the lower classes. Hence, the **exclusion clause** was inserted into the Rowing Association's rulebook. The exclusion clause was a device by high-minded administrators to exclude manual workers (the lower class) from their sport. Written in 1882, it was dropped within ten years when the definition of a professional became someone who earned money from rowing.		

4	Athletics	By the 1850s, most major cities had a running track, and athletics meetings attracted large crowds of Victorian spectators. The Amateur Athletics Club (established in 1866 by ex-public school and university men keen to promote rational athletics and sportsmanship) adopted the exclusion clause of the Rowing Association. The Amateur Athletic Association was formed in 1880.

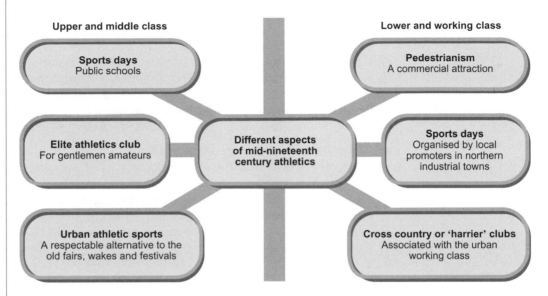

Fig. 1.12 The various aspects of athletics operating by the last quarter of the nineteenth century.

		The modern Olympic Movement: Baron Pierre de Coubertin established the modern Olympic Games in 1896. Impressed with the worthy ethics of late-nineteenth century English public schools, he sought to foster athleticism as well as patriotism for, and friendship between, nations. The Games were male-dominated and strictly amateur.
5	Association Football	The Football Association was formed in 1863 by ex-public schoolboys from Oxford and Cambridge, thereby forcing an official split between the dribbling game (favoured by Charterhouse) and the handling game (favoured by Rugby School). Unlike gentlemen amateurs, working-class players could not afford to take unpaid time from work to play. **Broken-time payments** were therefore sometimes made to outstanding working-class players to compensate for loss of earnings. This practice was looked down on by amateur **Corinthians** (ex-public school amateur games players, who stressed sportsmanship and fair play), and led to professionalism in both Association Football and rugby when, in 1895, the Northern Union split away from the south. When the football league was established in 1888, professionalism was finally and officially accepted. As a reflection of changing society, Association Football became the game of the working class. The popularity of the game can be attributed to many factors, including:

KEY WORDS

Broken-time payments

Corinthians

		• its simplicity • increased free time (especially Saturday half day) from 1870 • improved transport and communications • the affordability of gate money for working class males • the large numbers of local spectators who needed a focus • its potential for creating heroes • its potential for establishing community solidarity • increased literacy and the popular press
6	Cricket	Cricket is another game that had a strict class divide. While amateur players and organisers respected the skills of cricket professionals, they kept the paid men firmly in their place. For example, a professional would never captain a team; they ate separately; travelled separately; entered the field of play from a different door and had their names printed differently in programmes to underline their supposed inferior social position.
7	Lawn tennis	Lawn tennis was invented by and for the middle class, and its development reflects the growth of the urban middle class of late-nineteenth century Britain. Major Walter Wingfield patented and sold the game, which was to become the hallmark of every fashionable upper-middle-class garden. Later tennis clubs were formed and, later still, the lower classes had the opportunity to play in public parks. Lawn tennis had a role to play in the emancipation of women: • It was a social occasion. • Being physical, it helped to break down prevailing social attitudes about the role and status of women. • It was physical but did not require over-exertion or perceived unfemininity. • It did not require special dress. • Women could mix with men in an acceptable social setting. • It was private – high hedges and/or walls kept the party away from the prying eyes of the lower classes.

 CHECK !

Go back to the overview diagrams on pp. 2 and 18. If you are satisfied with your knowledge and understanding, tick off the sections that you have revised so far. If you are not satisfied, then revisit those sections and refer to the pages in the 'Need to know more?'

Section 4: *The development of drill, physical training and physical education in elementary schools*

Section overview

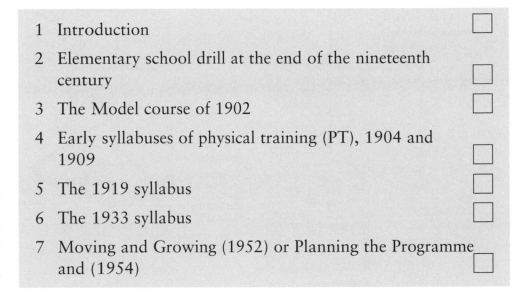

1 Introduction ☐

2 Elementary school drill at the end of the nineteenth century ☐

3 The Model course of 1902 ☐

4 Early syllabuses of physical training (PT), 1904 and 1909 ☐

5 The 1919 syllabus ☐

6 The 1933 syllabus ☐

7 Moving and Growing (1952) or Planning the Programme and (1954) ☐

Tick the box when you are satisfied with your level of knowledge and understanding for each topic within this section.

NEED TO KNOW MORE?

For further information on the development of drill, physical training and physical education in elementary schools, see pp. 55–64 in *Advanced PE for OCR: A2*.

HOT TIPS

It is important to be able to compare objectives, content and methodology over time – exam questions will often ask for this information.

HOT TIPS

It is important for your synoptic work to be able to compare the past (historical) with the present (contemporary).

KEY WORDS

Board schools

Objectives

Content

Methodology

1 Introduction

In this section you will revise the physical activity of junior age children who attended **board schools** (state schools that opened as a result of the Forster Education Act of 1870). You will remember:

- the **objectives** – aims or intentions of a lesson or syllabus; for example, physical or military fitness
- the **content** – the subject matter or activities taught in the lesson; for example, weapons drill or games skills
- the **methodology** – the teaching style used for delivery; for example, command or problem-solving.

These elements all developed over time which reflected, among other things, changing social conditions, educational thought and the training of specialist teachers.

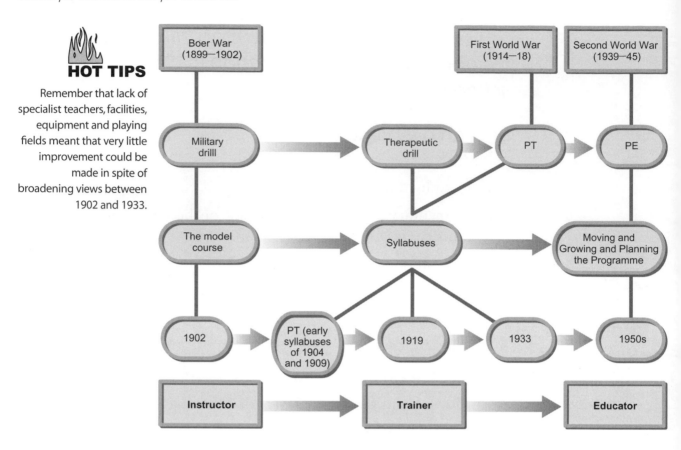

HOT TIPS

Remember that lack of specialist teachers, facilities, equipment and playing fields meant that very little improvement could be made in spite of broadening views between 1902 and 1933.

Fig. 1.13 Twentieth-century developments in state elementary schools.

KEY WORDS

Swedish gymnastics

Boer War

Colonel Fox

Non-commissioned officers

Therapeutic

Physical training

Open or problem-solving tasks

Decentralised/centralised

At the end of the nineteenth century, lessons might have included some military drill and perhaps even some games with **Swedish gymnastics** (a system of free-standing exercises created by Ling in the late 1800s to benefit the whole body systematically).

2 Elementary school drill at the end of the nineteenth century

Due to Britain's poor performance against South Africa in the **Boer War** (1899–1902) much prestige was lost and the War Office imposed a system of military drill called the Model course to redress the situation. **Colonel Fox**, a long-serving army officer, was appointed to ensure its adoption by schools. The Model course included marching, free-standing exercises and dummy weapons drill. Lessons were directed by army **non-commissioned officers** (NCOs). These were low-ranking personnel who had little interest in or knowledge of child development and whose involvement was therefore unbeneficial. Overall, this was a backward step.

3 The Model course of 1902

This was followed in 1904 and 1909 by **therapeutic drill**, which was more beneficial and health-giving than pure military drill. Dr George Newman, who had been appointed as Chief Medical Officer within the Board of Education, was influential in the adoption of this more health-giving approach.

4. Early syllabuses of physical training (PT), 1904 and 1909

Next came **physical training**, which consisted of Swedish exercises, gymnastics, drills, general activity exercises and games for the development and health of the body.

5 The 1919 syllabus

In retrospect, the 1933 syllabus of physical training is regarded as the main transition between what had gone before and what was yet to come. It was a detailed, high-quality and highly respected syllabus and the last to be published under the direction of Dr Newman.

6 The 1933 syllabus

Moving and Growing (1952) and Planning the Programme (1954) were innovative in their approach. They were child-centred, and included **open or problem solving tasks** that could be answered in a variety of ways. Lessons based on these documents were more **decentralised** than what had gone before. A **centralised** lesson has the teacher using an instructional style with all the children answering the same task in unison. A decentralised lesson has the teacher as a guide, with children working at their own pace answering tasks in an individual way.

7 Moving and Growing (1952) and Planning the Programme (1954)

Fig. 1.14 Pathway to the mid-nineteenth century.

KEY WORDS

Board schools

Important points/background information
- In 1866, the army rejected 380 out of each 1000 recruits on physical grounds.
- Board schools (state schools) established by the Forster Education Act 1870. Previously, the education of the poor had been a parish responsibility.
- School attendance became compulsory for children aged between five and ten years.
- By 1899, the school leaving age was raised to twelve years.
- By 1900, there had been great progress in terms of provision.
- Restricted space for play and physical exercise.
- Many schools in industrial towns had no playing facilities.

Influences
- The work of European gymnastic teachers, including Guts Muths and Jahn (Germany) and Ling (Sweden), as well as the Briton, A. Maclaren.

2 Elementary school drill
The end of the nineteenth century

Often built to look like churches, board schools had only small playgrounds and no playing fields.

Also note
- Lack of equipment other than staves (sticks) for dummy weapons drill.

Objectives
- Fitness for army recruits
- Discipline
- To do for working-class children what games was doing for public school boys

Content
- 1870 – military drill
- 1890s – Swedish drill
- 1900 – the Board of Education stated that games were a suitable alternative to Swedish drill

Methodology
- Authoritarian/Command-response
- Taught by army non-commissioned officers (NCOs) in 1870s
- Taught by qualified class teachers in 1890s

Fig. 1.15 Elementary school drill at the end of the nineteenth century.

Important points/background information
- Military needs became more powerful than educational theory.
- A backward step educationally with Swedish drill, innovation and a therapeutic approach abandoned.
- Condemned by progressives and supporters of the Swedish system.
- Girls and boys instructed together.
- Failed to cater for different ages and/or genders.
- Children treated as soldiers.
- Taught by army NCOs (or teachers who had been trained by them).
- Dull and repetitive – but cheap.
- Large numbers in small spaces.
- Set against backdrop of poor diets, bad housing and other forms of social deprivation.
- It lowered the status of the subject.

Influences
- Imposed as a result of Britain's poor performance in the Boer War.
- Produced and imposed by Colonel Fox of the War Office (not Education Department).

3 The Model course 1902

Massed drill in the school yard around 1902.

Also note
❝ It is important therefore that the short time claimed for physical training should be devoted wholly to useful exercises. No part of that time should be wasted on what is merely spectacular or entertaining, but every exercise should have its peculiar purpose and value in a complete system framed to develop all parts of the body. (*Model Course of Physical Training*, 1902) ❞

Objectives
- Fitness (for military service)
- Training in handling of weapons
- Discipline

Content
- Military drill
- Exercises
- Weapon training
- Deep breathing

Methodology
- Command-response (for example, 'Attention', 'Stand at ease', 'Marching, about turn'.)
- Group response/no individuality
- In ranks

Fig. 1.16 The Model course, 1902.

Important points/background information
- Revisions of the 1902 Model course.
- School medical service established within the Board of Education in 1908, 'which identified the necessity of raising the general standard of physical health among the children of the poor' (H. L. Fisher, House of Commons, 1918).
- A compromise between military drill and Swedish exercises.
- 1909 – local authorities required to train teachers to deliver the syllabuses.
- Emphasis on exercise in the open air and the use of suitable clothing.
- Still large numbers and poor facilities.

Influences
- Dr George Newman appointed as Chief Medical Officer within the Board of Education.
- As a medical man, he was interested in the health-giving/therapeutic effects of exercise.

HOT TIPS

Note the role of Dr George Newman in overseeing the publication of three Board of Education syllabuses between 1909 and 1933.

4 Early syllabuses of physical training (PT) 1904 and 1909

The early 1900s.

Also note

❛ The purpose of physical training is not to produce gymnasts, but to promote and encourage the health and development of the body. ❜ (Dr George Newman)

Objectives
- 1909 – therapeutic effects of exercise (with emphasis on respiration, circulation, posture)
- Obedience
- Discipline
- Enjoyment
- Alertness, decision-making, control of mind over body

Content
- 1909 – more Swedish in character with recreative aspects to relieve dullness, tedium and monotony of former lesson
- Dancing steps/simple games
- Danish and rhythmic swinging exercises

Methodology
- 1904 – 109 'tables' of exercises for teachers to follow
- 1909 – reduced to 71 'tables'
- Still formal
- Still in ranks with marching and 'free-standing' exercises
- Still unison response to commands
- A kinder approach by teachers
- Some freedom of choice for teachers

Fig. 1.17 Early syllabuses of physical training (PT), 1904 and 1900.

Important points/background information
- Set against the huge loss of life in the First World War and huge loss of life in post-war flu epidemic.
- The syllabus was progressive in terms of its broader content and child-centred appoach.

Influences
- Dr George Newman still influential and eager to fight off accusations that PT was to blame for the lack of fitness of the working class.
- Newman also stressed the benefits of recreative activities for the rehabilitation of injured soldiers.
- The Fisher Education Act 1918 promoted holiday and school camps, school playing fields and school swimming baths.

| 5 The syllabus 1919 |

The style of free-standing exercises still recommended in the 1919 syllabus.

Also note
- The first 'child-centred' syllabus.
- Broader content than 1902/1904/1909.
- But some older teachers stayed with their old ways.

Objectives
- Enjoyment and play for the under 7s
- Therapeutic work for the over 7s

Content
- The exercises and 'positions' the same as 1909
- Special section of games for the under 7s
- Not less than half the lesson on 'general activity exercises' – active free movement, including small games and dancing

Methodology
- More freedom for teachers and pupils
- Less formality

Fig. 1.18 The syllabus, 1919.

Important points/background information
- The industrial depression of the 1930s left many of the working class unemployed (no state benefits were yet available).
- A watershed between the syllabuses of the past and the physical education of the future.
- This syllabus had one section for the under elevens and one for the over elevens.

Influences
- The Hadow Report of 1926 identified the need to differentiate between ages for physical training.
- Dr George Newman – this was the last syllabus to be published under his direction.

6 Syllabus of physical training 1933

Emphasis on skills and posture.

Also note
- A detailed, high-quality and highly respected syllabus.
- Still set out in a series of 'tables' from which teachers planned their lessons.
- 'The ultimate test by which every system of physical training should be judged [is] to be found in the posture and general carriage of the children' (1933 syllabus).
- Newman stated that good nourishment, effective medical inspection and treatment and hygienic surroundings were all necessary for good health as well as 'a comprehensive system of physical training … for the normal healthy development of the body [and] for the correction of inherent or acquired defects'.

Objectives
- Physical fitness
- Therapeutic results
- Good physique
- Good posture
- Development of mind and body (holistic aims)

Content
- Athletics, gymnastic and games skills
- Group work

Methodology
- Still direct style for the majority of the lesson
- Some decentralised parts to the lesson
- Group work/tasks throughout
- Encouragement of special clothing/kit
- 5 × 20-minute lessons a week recommended
- Used many schools' newly built gymnasia
- Outdoor lessons recommended for health benefits

Fig. 1.19 Syllabus of physical training, 1933.

Important points/background information
- The (Butler) Education Act 1944 aimed to ensure equality of educational opportunity.
- It also required local authorities to provide playing fields for all schools.
- School leaving age was raised to fifteen years.
- These syllabuses should be viewed in the context of overall expansion of physical activities in schools.
- Intended to replace the under elevens section of the 1933 syllabus.

Influences
- The Second World War, which required 'thinking' soldiers, and the subsequent perceived need for increasingly 'thinking' children.
- Assault course obstacle equipment, influenced apparatus design.
- Modern educational dance methods influenced the creative/movement approach.
- An experiment in Halifax, which rehabilitated children with disabilities by encouraging individual interpretation of open tasks, with no pre-set rhythm or timing. This influenced the problem-solving approach.

7 1) Moving and Growing;   2) Planning the Programme
(1952)   (1954)

An apparatus lesson in the 1950s.

Also note
- The extensive post-war rebuilding programme lead to an expansion of facilities.

Objectives
- Physical, social and cognitive skills
- Variety of experiences
- Enjoyment
- Personal satisfaction
- Increased involvement for all

Content
- Agility exercises; gymnastics, dance and games skills
- Swimming
- Movement to music

Methodology
- Child-centred and enjoyment orientated
- Progressive
- Teacher guidance rather than direction
- Problem-solving/creative/exploratory/discovery
- Individual interpretation of tasks
- Using full apparatus (cave, ropes, bars, boxes, mats, and so on)

Fig. 1.20 1 Moving and Growing, 1952; 2 Planning the Programme, 1954.

CHECK !

Go back to the overview diagrams on pp. 1, 2 and 25. If you are satisfied with you knowledge and understanding, tick off the sections that you have revised so far. If you are not satisfied, then revisit those sections and refer to the pages in the 'Need to know more?'

Exam practice

1 Identify *two* characteristics of popular recreation and explain how each of them reflected pre-industrial British society. **(2 marks)**

2 What were the functions of pre-industrial wakes and fairs and what types of activities would they include? **(4 marks)**

3 Why was pedestrianism so popular in pre-industrial Britain? **(4 marks)**

4 Describe the nature of public school sports and pastimes in stage one of development before the reforms of liberal headmasters such as Dr Thomas Arnold. **(4 marks)**

5

'It's more than a game. It's an institution.'

'It merges the individual in the eleven.'

'Football and cricket … are such much better games than fives or hare-and-hounds.'

'The discipline and reliance on one another … is so valuable.'

Fig. 1.21 Tom Brown in conversation with Arthur and the young master.

5 (a) What did Tom mean about cricket being an institution? **(1 mark)**
  (b) Why were football and cricket thought to be better games than fives or hare-and-hounds? **(1 mark)**
  (c) Comment on the social relationship between the three people in the picture. **(1 mark)**

6 How did ex-public school and university boys influence the local, national and international spread of sports and games? **(3 marks)**

7 Outline how the Industrial Revolution restricted opportunities for the lower class to take part in their traditional sports and pastimes in the first half of the nineteenth century and how opportunities improved in the second half of the century. **(6 marks)**

8 Account for the growth and popularity of Association Football as 'the People's Game' in late nineteenth-century Britain. **(5 marks)**

9 With reference to objectives, content and methodology, identify key features of each of the following:
  • The 1902 Model course.
  • The 1933 syllabus.
  • Physical education in the 1950s (Moving and Growing/Planning the Programme). **(9 marks)**

Now go to p. 168 to check your answers.

Chapter 2 **Comparative studies**

Chapter overview

1 Cultural background and sporting history of the USA ☐

2 Cultural background of France ☐

3 Physical education in schools (France) ☐

4 Ethnic sports and cultural links (France) ☐

5 Mass participation (Sport for All) (France) ☐

6 Sport and the pursuit of excellence (France) ☐

7 Outdoor education and outdoor recreation (France) ☐

8 Cultural background of Australia ☐

9 Physical education in schools and colleges (Australia) ☐

10 Ethnic sports and new games (Australia) ☐

11 Mass participation in sport (Australia) ☐

12 Sport and the pursuit of excellence (Australia) ☐

13 Outdoor education and outdoor recreation (Australia) ☐

Tick the box when you are satisfied with your level of knowledge and understanding for each section within this chapter.

Section 1: *Cultural background and sporting history of the USA*

KEY WORDS

Indigenous Colonialism

NEED TO KNOW MORE?

See pages 65–67 and 70–72 in *Advanced PE for OCR: A2*

1 Introduction

Due to the abundance of material already available on sport in the USA, we have chosen to provide detailed coverage of France and Australia – topics with which students may be less familiar and confident – as well as a succinct summary of sport in the USA. However, the USA is just as important as France and Australia in this syllabus.

For more detail on sport in the USA, please refer to the pupil book – *Advanced PE for OCR A2*.

A brief overview of US history

Before European settlement the indigenous population of North America comprised Indian tribes who played a game called baggatoway. Baggatoway survived colonialism and developed into lacrosse which is popular in the USA today.

HOT TIPS

The changing mainstream culture (as it developed as a result of large-scale immigration) rejected cricket. Today it is an exclusive game played by few in the USA.

- During the seventeenth century, the Dutch, Spanish, French and British set up separate colonies
- The dominant colonists were British who continued to play their sports from home. Cricket was popular.
- North America was beginning to evolve into a multicultural society which would later be dominated by White Anglo-Saxon **Protestant (WASPS)**.
- The Declaration of Independence (on the 4th July 1776) marked the birth of the USA. Links with the UK were severed in a policy of isolation.

HOT TIPS

Isolation changed the culture of the USA and this change was reflected in sport.

Sport in the USA

Sport is one of the most popular cultural practices. It is associated with a 'win at all cost' ethic that permeates both sport and society in the USA. The dominant ideologies of the country comprise the 'American Dream', capitalism, opportunity, liberty and freedom.

HOT TIPS

By comparison consider the relationship of Australia with the UK.

The 'Big Four' sports in the USA are shown in the table below:

Classification	USA 'Big Four Sports'
Adaptations	American Football (Grid Iron), Baseball
Adoptions	Ice Hockey
Inventions	Basketball

HOT TIPS

Exam questions carrying the higher marks will often ask about the culture of a given country. Consider why sport in the USA is regarded as the last frontier.

KEY WORDS

Frontier

HOT TIPS

Be aware of the Frontier spirit and how it has shaped USA ideology.

KEY WORDS

Hegemony

HOT TIPS

Consider why only soccer in the UK approaches the level of commercialism achieved by the USA 'Big Four' sports

NEED TO KNOW MORE?

See pages 89–91 in *Advanced PE for OCR: A2*.

NEED TO KNOW MORE?

See pages 73–81 in *Advanced PE for OCR: A2*.

- These sports are multi-million dollar industries committed to entertain. They are driven by commercialism.
- These sports are required to be sensational and are often associated with images of aggression and violence.

Sport and the Pursuit of Excellence

- High school is regarded as a centre for sporting excellence
- The coach is responsible for results and is employed on a 'hire and fire' basis
- Students are motivated by the incentive of a college sport scholarship
- College (the US universities) sports are organised on a commercial basis
- Players (students) do not receive direct payment but have the benefit of the scholarship and the incentive of the Pro-draft

Discrimination in sport

- The **WASPS** tend to be the controlling hegemonic group
- Ethnic minority groups have experienced discrimination in sport but were given more opportunity to participate from the mid 20th Century onwards
- Sports success is important to ethnic minority groups in the USA
- There is still evidence of 'stacking' and 'centrality' in USA sport

Mass participation

- There is a well established jogging and gym culture in the USA
- There is limited opportunity for adult mass sports participation
- Little League participation exists for children

Physical education in the USA

- As with most administrations in the USA, education operates in a decentralised system.
- The teacher is made very accountable in Physical Education and control lies with the School Board and the District Superintendent.
- Measures are in place to ensure equality in Physical Education.
- There is a heavy emphasis on fitness and direct skill learning, all of which is assessed practically.
- A crisis currently exists as compulsory daily Physical Education is disappearing from High School lesson plans.
- Physical Education for Progress (PEP) is a programme designed to address this crisis.

HOT TIPS

For synoptic questions compare the opportunity for mass participation in UK, France, and Australia.

NEED TO KNOW MORE?

See pages 94-96 in *Advanced PE for OCR: A2*.

NEED TO KNOW MORE?

See pages 97-99 in *Advanced PE for OCR: A2*.

NEED TO KNOW MORE?

For further information on the cultural background of France, see pp. 101–5 in *Advanced PE for OCR: A2*.

HOT TIPS

Exam questions carrying the higher marks will often ask about the culture of a given country.

HOT TIPS

In the exam you could be asked to link the major ideologies with sporting topics.

Outdoor Recreation and Outdoor Education

- There is great geographical potential for outdoor activities in a vast country possessing genuine wilderness.
- USA was the first country to establish National Parks. These are under Federal control.
- Outward Bound and Summer Camp opportunities exist for children.
- Summer Camps offer a diversity of activities for children.
- Accessibility to the best camps is financially determined
- The Summer Camp system strongly reflects the American capitalist system.

Section 2: *Cultural background of France*

1 Introduction ☐

2 Geographic and demographic variables ☐

3 Education in France ☐

Tick the box when you are satisfied with your level of knowledge and understanding for each topic within this section.

1 Introduction

The approach to sport and physical education in France is strongly influenced by the national culture.

French ideologies of nationalism, militarism, intellectualism and naturalism influence national culture.

France has a history of national triumph and despair brought about through revolution, empire and military occupation.

- A legacy of the revolution (1789) impacts upon French culture today. The patriotic slogan of the revolution, **Liberté, Egalitié et Fraternité** means:
- At the time of the revolution, France became known as the 'land of asylum' and began a long tradition of accommodating 'foreigners'. The policy of 'assimilation' has integrated ethnic minorities into society and this has enhanced French international prowess in sport in the latter part of the twentieth century.
- France consolidated its Empire in the late 1800s and became an influential nation.

- Heavy losses in the First World War proved to be a serious national setback.
- Demoralising German occupation in the Second World War emphasised the geographical vulnerability of France.
- The emergency **Vichy government** tried to restore patriotic pride through sport.
- The collapse of the French Empire in the post-war period and failure in the 1956 Olympic Games marked a low point in the history of the country.
- President de Gaulle (who became president in 1958) restored the fortunes of the French nation.

HOT TIPS

Through economic investment de Gaulle made sport the rallying point for renewed French nationalism.

2 Geographic and demographic variables

- Three climatic types exist in France.
- There are three high-level mountain ranges.
- France covers more than twice the area of the UK but has the same population.
- Paris is densely populated but the remainder of France is considered rural.
- There is an economic dependence on agriculture, particularly viticulture in the south.

HOT TIPS

Understand the impact of history and geography on French sport, physical education and outdoor education and recreation.

3 Education in France

- **Intellectualism**, a key feature of French ideology, is a traditional societal value.
- The National Education Ministry controls most schools.
- The **Baccalaureate** examination can involve PE and gives a qualification equivalent to A2 or AVCE in the UK.

Decentralisation in education

- Since the 1990s, the French government has decentralised the administration of education.
- The National Education Ministry has devolved decision-making responsibilities to regional and local authorities.
- There are now 22 regional departments, sub-divided into 96 local departments.
- Decentralisation has made it possible for each school to have flexibility to deliver a curriculum that is most relevant to the geographical area that it serves.

NEED TO KNOW MORE?

For further information on education in France, see pp. 103–9 in *Advanced PE for OCR: A2*.

KEY WORDS

Intellectualism

Baccalaureate

✔ CHECK !

Go back to the overview diagrams on pp. 36 ad 39. If you are satisfied with your knowledge and understanding, tick off the sections that you have revised so far. If you are not satisfied, then revisit those sections and refer to the pages in the 'Need to know more?'

Section 3: *Physical education in schools (France)*

NEED TO KNOW MORE?

For further information on physical education in schools in France, see pp. 106–10 in *Advanced PE for OCR: A2*.

HOT TIPS

Physical education in France is now perceived to contribute significantly to the development of the whole person. This brings it into line with the values acknowledged in the UK.

HOT TIPS

Be aware of the change in attitude towards PE in France

NEED TO KNOW MORE?

For further information on assessment in schools, see pp. 107–8 in *Advanced PE for OCR: A2*.

| 1 | Introduction | ☐ |
| 2 | School sport in France | ☐ |

Tick the box when you are satisfied with your level of knowledge and understanding for each topic within this section.

1 Introduction

The attitude toward physical education in France has reversed significantly since the end of the twentieth century. Previously the subject lacked status as a curriculum element and teachers were considered inferior to those delivering 'cultural' subjects.

Reasons for a lack of status:

- A strong military link existed with the subject.
- The subject was regarded as non-intellectual.
- Responsibility for PE was with the Secretary for Youth and Sport while other subjects were controlled by the Minister for Education.
- Centrally controlled programmes were not delivered effectively.

Ways in which attitudes have reversed and the status has increased:

- The subject is perceived to have holistic educative value.
- Control is now with the Ministry of National Education.
- Teacher training is now of a high standard.
- The government has committed to a policy to upgrade physical education.
- Physical education is now associated with cognitive and social development.
- A structured programme exists in primary schools.
- There is a clear progression through National Curriculum to the Baccalaureate, which now includes some written assignments.
- The subject is now inspected at all levels every two years.

2 School sport in France

Sport has always been regarded favourably in French schools as it has high status in society.

Union Nationale du Sport Scholaire (UNSS)	Sporting sections	Primary sports schools
The UNSS delivers sport to all secondary school children	Sporting sections have a mission to develop excellence	Provide experiences in physical education down to pupils aged six
This ensures a broad participation base	Sections are specialist departments within the school	Regional departments allocate finance
It is part of the Multi-Sport Federation	Sections select children with high sporting potential	The purpose is to develop talent, not to produce champions
The UNSS is funded and centrally controlled by the government	Academic progress cannot be compromised	Primary sport schools are non-selective
Competitive sport is also a priority	Training schedules are arranged around timetabled study	Gymnastics appears to be the main focus
Specialist coaches operate to develop excellence	Specialist coaches work with children	Volleyball, basketball and handball are also offered
UNSS representation goes up to school international standard	Sections are located in all regions	Indoor facilities are of high standard
Community facilities in a system of joint provision	All sections receive government funding	Specialist coaches work alongside physical education teachers
Wednesday afternoon sports fixtures are arranged		The timetabled day is extended and academic study integrated

USEP (Sporting Union of the Primary School) has the responsibility of overseeing the organisation of sport in the primary sector.

 CHECK !

Go back to the overview diagrams on pp. 36 and 41. If you are satisfied with your knowledge and understanding, tick off the sections that you have revised so far. If you are not satisfied, then revisit those sections and refer to the pages in the 'Need to know more?'

Section 4: *Ethnic sports and cultural links (France)*

Section overview

> 1 Ethnic games ☐
>
> 2 Characteristics and functions of ethnic games ☐

NEED TO KNOW MORE?

For further information on ethnic sports and cultural links in France, see pp. 110–12 in *Advanced PE for OCR: A2.*

Tick the box when you are satisfied with your level of knowledge and understanding for each topic within this section.

1 Ethnic games

An ethnic game is one that is confined to a small geographical area (usually rural and remote). Ethnic games:

- have only local significance
- can take place on a daily basis, for example churn carrying in central France
- can be part of a large annual festival like the Basque 'Strongman' sports festival.

HOT TIPS

For synoptic questions, be able to compare French with UK ethnic games.

Link ethnic games with regionalism and nationalism.

Examples of ethnic games in France:

Breton wrestling	Basque sports festival	Bull fighting
Confined to Brittany in the north-west of the country	The six Basque provinces meet annually for a rural games festival	The French Basques engage in bull fighting
Dates back to the 1300s	'Strongman' sports dominate the programme	A popular festival event but a brutal spectacle
Bound by its own traditional rules	The winning team claims only the traditional beret as a trophy	Opposition from the French Animal Rights League

2 Characteristics and functions of ethnic games

Characteristics	Functions
Location. Rural, remote and isolated regions	**Champion**. Local pride in the champion
Structure. Simple rules, unsophisticated activities	**Unity**. Creates rural unity
Timing. Annual festivals or regular participation	**Distraction**. Boredom relief during manual jobs
Origins. Historical roots with traditional customs	**Recreation**. Opportunity for fun and gambling

Characteristics	Functions
Availability. Confined to one area	**Culture**. Sub-cultural identity of the community
Reflection. Of local jobs and the working environment	**Celebration**. A form of spectacle and entertainment
	Political. Ethnic groups appeased
	Commercialism. Commercial opportunities
Proof of manliness. Is both a characteristic and a function of an ethnic game	

The table above applies to all ethnic games whether their location is in France or UK.

✔ CHECK !

Go back to the overview diagrams on pp. 36 and 43. If you are satisfied with your knowledge and understanding, tick off the sections that you have revised so far. If you are not satisfied, then revisit those sections and refer to the pages in the 'Need to know more?'

Section 5: *Mass participation (Sport for All) (France)*

1   Government policies relating to sport ☐

2   The rise of 'new' sports ☐

Tick the box when you are satisfied with your level of knowledge and understanding for each topic within this section.

1 Government policies relating to sport

Sport has increasing importance in French society. From 1963 to 2003 club membership has risen sixfold, stimulated by government policy:

- President de Gaulle's Economic Plan of 1958 did much to increase mass participation.
- De Gaulle made sport the rallying point for the revival of national pride.
- France was one of the first countries to provide state funding for sport.
- In 2003, 50 per cent of French people said they took part in sport.

President de Gaulle's Economic Plan for sport comprised seven major strategies to address the dual issues of participation and developing excellence.

HOT TIPS

A popular exam question focuses on the structure and function of ethnic games.

HOT TIPS

La boule does not fit with the description of an ethnic game. It is not restricted to one area and is even played in England. However, the origins and traditions of this street game are firmly rooted in France.

NEED TO KNOW MORE?

For further information on mass participation in France, see pp. 113–18 in *Advanced PE for OCR: A2*.

HOT TIPS

These strategies could be the focus of an examination question.

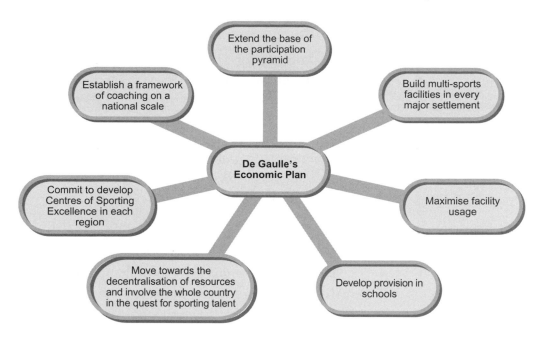

In common with the international Sport for All policy, the French have *Sport pour Tous*.

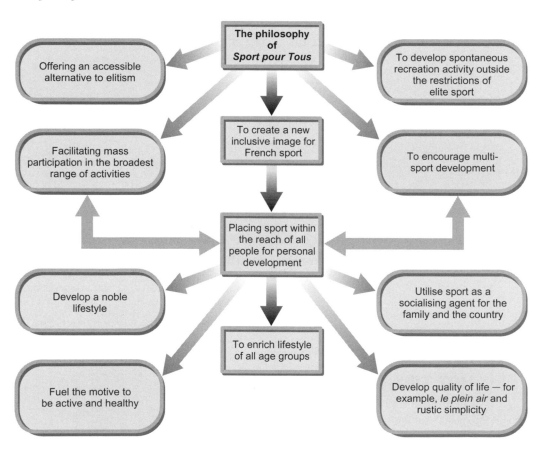

Fig. 2.01 Philosophy of *Sport pour Tous*.

Funding

- The Ministry for Youth and Sport manages the National Sports Fund (Fund Nationale pour le Developement du Sport – FNDS).
- This is used to promote growth at grass root levels and provide equipment for regional sports clubs.
- The fund is supported through taxation and a small percentage of profits made by public companies.
- The French National Lottery has provided a significant financial contribution since 1985.

Finance is distributed through five sporting federations.

1 *Sports Olympiques* (Olympic Federation).
2 *Sports Non-Olympiques* (Non-Olympic Federation).
3 *Multi-Sports Federation* (associated federations).
4 *Scholaires et Universitaires* (School and University Federation).
5 *Federation Française Handisports* (FFH) (athletes with disabilities).

2 The rise of 'new' sports

Although golf and tennis have historical roots, they are classified as 'new' sports because of twentieth-century development and are new compared with the 'old' ethnic games.

Golf:

- is experiencing increased popularity brought about through improved provision and accessibility
- ranks as the ninth most popular game in France
- is becoming a significant tourist attraction with considerable potential for expansion.

You need to be aware of the geographical and cultural advantages that are stimulating the growth of golf and making France an attractive golf venue.

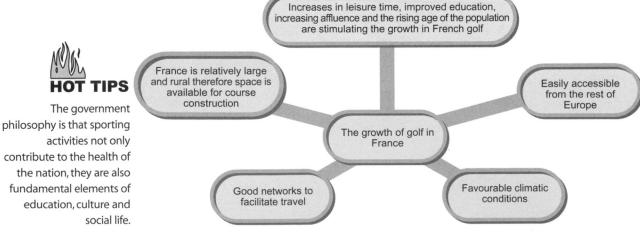

Increases in leisure time, improved education, increasing affluence and the rising age of the population are stimulating the growth in French golf

France is relatively large and rural therefore space is available for course construction

Easily accessible from the rest of Europe

The growth of golf in France

Good networks to facilitate travel

Favourable climatic conditions

Tennis is the second most popular game in France (over one million players).

- High-class facilities can be found throughout France.
- Provision for tennis endorses the success of government investment.
- The climate is conducive to outdoor tennis.
- France was included as an international venue in 1925 and, today, the French Open Tournament attracts large audiences.

 CHECK !

Go back to the overview diagrams on pp. 36 and 44. If you are satisfied with your knowledge and understanding, tick off the sections that you have revised so far. If you are not satisfied, then revisit those sections and refer to the pages in the 'Need to know more?'

Section 6: *Sport and the pursuit of excellence (France)*

Section overview

1 INSEP ☐
2 Amateur sport and nationalism ☐
   - Tour de France
   - Rugby
   - Association football

NEED TO KNOW MORE?

For further information on sport and the pursuit of excellence in France, see pp. 119–24 in *Advanced PE for OCR: A2*.

Tick the box when you are satisfied with your level of knowledge and understanding for each topic within this section.

1 INSEP

Function of INSEP

- Produces elite performers and is also the major sports education centre in France.
- A multi-sport centre of excellence catering for 25 different sports.

- Makes decision concerning funding allocations to the sports federations.
- Selects the athletes who will attend for training.
- Is ultimately responsible for the development of French sport.

In addition to INSEP, there are five national state-run sporting institutes in France specialising in their own field.

National Equestrian School (ENE), Samur, Loire	National School of Sailing (ENV), Saint Pierre Quilberon	National Altitude Centre (pre-Olympic complex), Font Romeu	National School of Cross-Country Skiing and Ski Jumping (ENSF), Chamonix	National School of Skiing and Mountaineering (ENSA), Chamonix (Mont Blanc)

Fig. 2.02 INSEP and the five specialist national institutes of France.

KEY WORDS

CREPS

- Approximately 25 per cent of the 3000 elite French athletes can be resident in these institutions at one time.
- The remainder attend one of the 22 regional sporting centres of excellence, called Centres d'Education Physique et Sporting (**CREPS**).
- The sporting federations select the young athletes who attend these centres.

2 Amateur sport and nationalism

NEED TO KNOW MORE?

For further information on amateur sport and nationalism, see pp. 121–3 in *Advanced PE for OCR: A2*.

- Historically, France is an enigma in terms of its stance on amateurism and professionalism.
- Baron de Courbertin resurrected the modern Olympic Games in 1896 as a strictly amateur enterprise.
- The Vichy government of 1942 abolished all professional sport.
- In both cases the amateur ethic supported the mission of nationalism.

Tour de France

Contrary to the amateur ethic, the Tour de France is the world's best-known professional cycle race. The motives underlying the event are for financial gain and are not totally nationalistic.

HOT TIPS

The last two points increase the opportunity for sponsorship and show solidarity with the European community.

- The scenic route taken provides excellent tourist publicity.
- The winner claims over 300,000 euros.
- Representation is organised on the basis of brand name sponsorship, not as teams representing their country.
- Each year the starting location varies.
- The race detours through some of France's neighbouring countries.

However, a flavour of nationalism is evident in the race as the finish in Paris is always the traditional sprint along the historic Champs-Elysées.

Rugby

Rugby has its roots in middle-class England, in the Home Nations and the British Empire. The game appears incongruous with the French culture.

- From the early twentieth century, the game was played throughout France.
- The heartland was and remains today in the viticulture regions in the south-west of the country.
- From the outset violence and payment of players conflicted strongly with the ethic of the amateur English Rugby Union.
- France was suspended from the Five Nations Championship in 1931.
- Rugby League emerged as a serious rival.
- The 'new code' could make legitimate payments and was never to be popular with the middle classes and the government in France.
- Lack of favour in high society ultimately led to the demise of 'League' in 1942 at the hands of the Vichy wartime government.
- It was decreed that a professional game could not be used as a rallying point for nationalism.
- Ironically, Rugby Union has an increasingly professional orientation.
- The success of the French Union team (2004) was a stimulant for nationalism.
- Today Rugby League in France is largely amateur and is marginalised.

Association football

- French law impedes the growth of an extravagant American-style sports business.
- Heavy taxation is inflicted on high-earning players, so players are seeking contracts outside France.
- France won the soccer World Cup in 1998 because the state funds sport at grass roots level, providing good facilities and coaching progression.
- Politicians would like to see more French soccer stars playing at home rather than abroad.

 CHECK !

Go back to the overview diagrams on pp. 36 and 47. If you are satisfied with your knowledge and understanding, tick off the sections that you have revised so far. If you are not satisfied, then revisit those sections and refer to the pages in the 'Need to know more?'

Section 7: *Outdoor education and outdoor recreation (France)*

Section overview

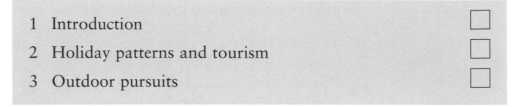

1 Introduction ☐
2 Holiday patterns and tourism ☐
3 Outdoor pursuits ☐

NEED TO KNOW MORE?

For further information on outdoor recreation and outdoor education in France, see pp. 124–8 *Advanced PE for OCR: A2.*

KEY WORDS

Le plein air

HOT TIPS

Activity holidays involving recreation activities in the outdoors are the fastest-growing element of the French tourist industry.

Tick the box when you are satisfied with your level of knowledge and understanding for each topic within this section.

1 Introduction

The concept of outdoor activities in France is expressed as *le plein air*, which reflects the ideology of naturalism.

- There are seven national parks in France under strict state control.
- 40 regional parks are distributed evenly throughout France.

2 Holiday patterns and tourism

General opportunities for outdoor activity participation are increasing for all ages.

- Centres de Vacances are holiday recreation centres offering activities and sports to all age groups.
- Village camps specialise in outdoor education for school children aged between 6 and 16.
- Vacances sans Frontières is one example of a large holiday business group that specialises in summer camp and outdoor activity provision.
- The Sports Camp is an alternative summer residential experience.
- The Outward Bound movement exists in France. It is called Hors Limites.

All residential camps are paid for by parents, which highlights a new societal trend. The concept of the French family vacation is changing, as some parents are now taking holidays alone while children attend summer camps.

HOT TIPS

Adults are more likely to organise their own activities, for example walking, hiking and cycling holidays.

HOT TIPS

An exam question could focus on outdoor provision and ask about the geographical potential for outdoor activities in France.

HOT TIPS

Remember questions awarding higher marks could examine one topic and ask the candidate to link the answer with the ideologies of the country.

3 Outdoor pursuits

Outdoor pursuits are taught to a high standard at the Chamonix Mountain Centre of Excellence and Le Centre Nationale des Sports de Plein Air.

Les Classes Transplantées programme is a primary school programme involving outdoor activities. It is government funded.

The major and most relevant transplantée classes in outdoor education are:

- *Classe de Neige*: downhill and cross-country skiing
- *Classe de Vert*: orienteering, hiking and expeditions in the forest
- *Classe de Mer*: sailing and other aquatic activities in the sea.

Fig. 2.03 Extreme outdoor pursuits

 CHECK !

Go back to the overview diagrams on pp. 36 and 50. If you are satisfied with your knowledge and understanding, tick off the sections that you have revised so far. If you are not satisfied, then revisit those sections and refer to the pages in the 'Need to know more?'

Section 8: *Cultural background of Australia*

Section overview

1 Introduction ☐
2 Indigenous peoples ☐
3 The first settlers ☐
4 Australian ideologies ☐

NEED TO KNOW MORE?

For further information on the cultural background of Australia, see pp. 128–32 in *Advanced PE for OCR: A2.*

Tick the box when you are satisfied with your level of knowledge and understanding for each topic within this section.

1 Introduction

KEY WORDS

Motherland

Australia became independent from the UK in 1901. Unlike the USA, Australia has maintained its links with the UK – referred to as the '**Motherland**'. Throughout Australia there is evidence of colonial roots; education, sports ethos and general traditions are very similar to those found in the UK today.

- Australia has a decentralised system of government which gives autonomy to each state.
- Consequently, local government differs significantly between the states and territories.
- From 1945 until the mid 1960s, the Australian government sponsored emigration from the UK (partly explaining why 95 per cent of the population is white and principally of British descent).
- Today over 150 nationalities co-exist in Australia and it is one of the most diverse nations.

The great size of Australia has impacted upon the culture of the nation.

- Distances involved made the widespread development of sport in the nineteenth century difficult.
- Good communication networks in the twentieth century and advanced technological communication of the twenty-first century have created accessibility and unity.

Australia has a small population of 19 million living in eight major cities which all have coastal locations.

2 Indigenous peoples

- The Aborigines are the indigenous people of Australia and Tasmania.
- They suffered badly during the period of white settlement from 1788.
- The 'white invaders' marginalised the Aborigines and a 'white Australia policy' was adopted.
- This policy was abolished in 1971 and a commitment made to multi-culturalism.
- Although Aboriginals make up only 2 per cent of the Australian population, they have been disproportionately successful in major sports like boxing, Rugby League and 'Aussie Rules'.

3 The first settlers

- The modern Australian nation was not built upon convict settlement.
- People seeking opportunity came later during the early nineteenth century to farm the land and dig for gold.

- The 'bush culture' emerged as some opportunists mirrored the frontier spirit of the USA.
- Among these migrants was an aspiring middle-class element from England who played sports and did much to shape the culture of Australia.
- Between 1862 and 1904, Melanesian and Polynesian workers were engaged as cheap labour. They helped to establish the beach culture and revolutionised swimming.
- The migrating British continued traditional sports from the 'old country'. Therefore cricket and rugby gained a firm foothold.

4 Australian ideologies

- A capitalist democratic society of the Western model.
- A strong egalitarian ethos prevails; for example, the slogan 'the land of the fair go'.
- Pluralism is a societal value; for example, multi-culturalism policy.
- A strong sense of nationalism exists in a young and ambitious culture.

 CHECK !

Go back to the overview diagrams on pp. 36 and 51. If you are satisfied with your knowledge and understanding, tick off the sections that you have revised so far. If you are not satisfied, then revisit those sections and refer to the pages in the 'Need to know more?'

Section 9: *Physical education in schools and colleges (Australia)*

1 Introduction ☐

2 Aussie Sport ☐

3 The organisation of inter-school sport in Victoria and Australia ☐

4 Selection policies ☐

NEED TO KNOW MORE?

For further information on physical education in schools and colleges in Australia, see pp. 133–9 in *Advanced PE for OCR: A2.*

Tick the box when you are satisfied with your level of knowledge and understanding for each topic within this section.

1 Introduction

Following a government enquiry in 1992 into declining standards of skill and fitness levels, changes have taken place in the delivery of sport and physical education in schools.

Victoria State responded to the enquiry by implementing the recommendations of the 1993 Monaghetti Review.

To improve the provision, physical education and sport education programmes were made compulsory for pupils up to Year 10.

Edith Cowan University in Western Australia presented a model – Sport Education and Physical Education Project (SEPEP) – as a suggested guide to the teaching of physical activities.

KEY WORDS

Australian Sports Commission (ASC)

- The **Australian Sports Commission (ASC)**, a government committee with responsibility for sport, funded the initial research.
- SEPEP provides a framework and is available to all throughout the Australian physical education system. It is not a national curriculum.
- Teachers are free to adapt and innovate their own programmes to suit their students.
- The government law was that all schools in Australia delivered 100 minutes' sport education and 100 minutes' physical education each week.
- The programme does not set out to produce excellence.
- A strong emphasis is placed on 'fair play'.
- In primary schools (Years 1–6), the **fundamental skills programme** (a compulsory physical education programme for primary children) was implemented.

HOT TIPS

A synoptic question could focus on the differences between Australian and UK sport and physical education in schools. Be aware that in Australia there is no national curriculum or inspection service and teachers are granted professional autonomy.

2 Aussie Sport

KEY WORDS

More Active Australia

Fundamental skills programme

- In 1982, the ASC saw a need to reinvigorate junior sport.
- A programme ('Aussie Sport') was designed comprising modified sports and mini-games played with adapted 'child friendly' equipment.
- The ASC withdrew funding in 1996; the Aussie Sport programme no longer exists.

3 The organisation of inter-school sport in Victoria and Australia

KEY WORDS

Game sense

Operating alongside physical education in the secondary school is the sports education programme.

- Pupils experience a different activity each term.
- Sports are initially played on an intra-school basis.

- Inter-schools competition is undertaken in the final three weeks of term, with the most successful schools qualifying for the district, zonal and eventually state finals.
- Six school sports associations – for example, VSSSA (Victoria) and QSSS (Queensland) – organise intra state competitions.
- School Sport Australia (SSA) is the overarching controlling body for school sport. It is an advisory council for the whole of the country.

Inter-school sport continues during Years 9–10, but traditional sports give way to **elective** activities (the equivalent of options in the UK).

- Sports coaches may be employed part-time.
- Senior pupils can elect to become sports leaders and become involved in administration, refereeing and coaching.

A further incentive for promising school performers is the possibility of selection for the Pacific School Games (PSG). In excess of 3000 abled and disabled primary and secondary school pupils will be involved in the 2005 Games.

4 Selection policies

- Sport Education in schools is non-elitist.
- Pupils who demonstrate a high level of talent are directed towards club participation in a scheme called 'sports linkage', which involves the school and club-sharing facilities.
- Head teachers have the authority to operate elitist programmes in single sports.

Assessment in physical education:

- Assessment in physical education from Years 7–10 is based on practical competence and attitude.
- Fitness standards are tested in secondary schools, leading to the Australian Fitness Education Award.
- The tests, designed by the **Australian Council for Health, Physical Education and Recreation**, apply to the whole of Australia and are concerned with personal improvement.

In Years 11 and 12 students take the High School Certificate (HSC) examination.

- Each state has a version of the HSC for example – the Victoria Certificate of Education (VCE).
- At VCE level, physical education is an elective subject and is assessed entirely on theoretical knowledge.

Teacher education:

- The Victoria School Sports Unit also commits to the training of teachers through in-service training – **Physical and Sport Education (PASE)** is a professional development programme.
- All professional development is financed by the government and delivered by ACHPER.

Exemplary schools:

- Teachers from these schools deliver professional development and share good practice with neighbouring institutions.

'Sports person in school' project:

- This project brings athletes into schools as role models to advise and supplement curriculum delivery.

- Celebrities must plan talks and workshops as part of the Athletes Career Education (ACE).
- These athletes may be sponsored by the **Victoria Institute of Sport (VIS)** (one of nine national centres of sports excellence).

Raising teacher profiles:

- Teachers raise their own profiles as role models by engaging in the 'Teachers' Games'.

Student awards for sport achievement and administration:

- The government offers regional awards for attainment and fair play and nominations are submitted for state awards.
- The de Courbertin awards are presented to students who have made outstanding contributions to administration, coaching and other important non-playing roles.

 CHECK !

Go back to the overview diagrams on pp. 36 and 53. If you are satisfied with your knowledge and understanding, tick off the sections that you have revised so far. If you are not satisfied, then revisit those sections and refer to the pages in the 'Need to know more?'

Section 10: *Ethnic sports and new games (Australia)*

Section overview

NEED TO KNOW MORE?

For further information on ethnic sports and new games, see pp. 140–2 in *Advanced PE for OCR: A2.*

1 Introduction	☐
2 The development of Australian football (Aussie Rules)	☐

Tick the box when you are satisfied with your level of knowledge and understanding for each topic within this section.

1 Introduction

- Games played by Aboriginal societies were functional, often focusing on survival.
- Sports also reflected the economic and cultural factors in society.
- Games improved fitness necessary for a hunter-gatherer existence.
- Competitions in tree climbing, spear and boomerang throwing, running, swimming and animal tracking were conducted within the group and on an inter-tribal basis.
- The Aborigines also played games for fun.
- It is thought that the Aboriginal game of marn-grook involved a leaping tactic copied as a marking strategy in what was to become Aussie Rules football.
- Aborigine numbers were decimated by 'white rule'.
- During the mid-twentieth century most had been placed into missions or assimilated into Australian society as low-paid workers with limited rights.
- The Aboriginal issue became a source of embarrassment, particularly as a commitment to multi-culturalism in 1971 had ended the 'white Australian policy'.
- By the 1990s, the government had granted land rights to the Aborigines.
- Standards of living and life expectancy remain incomparable with Australian people.

2 The development of Australian football (Aussie Rules)

There is strong evidence to support the claim that Aussie Rules is a genuine Australian game:

- Its origins involve a cross between an Aboriginal game and the football games which had begun to evolve in the English public schools in the early nineteenth century.
- Melbourne Rules extended to Victoria Rules and, eventually, Aussie Rules became a national sport with the title of Australian football.

KEY WORDS

Cornstalks

Several cultural factors shaped the game:

- It was originally designed to maintain the fitness of cricketers in winter.
- The Aborigines were included and contributed athleticism.

- The Irish gained renown for strength and ruggedness.
- The '**cornstalks**' (the name given to second-and third-generation Australians) brought skills strategies to the sport, along with the new manly image of 'frontier' Australia.
- Spectators also brought influence. The game appealed to all classes, endorsing the egalitarian nature of society.
- Teams comprise eighteen players with half forwards running 25 km during the course of a highly skilled game.
- Australian football requires six officials to cover the pitch.
- It has expanded due to twenty-first century commercialism.
- Fair play is a high priority.
- The Brownlow medal is presented to the best and fairest player each year.

Fig. 2.04 Australian football. 'Footy' has evolved rules, skills and tactics of its own and is now the game of the cosmopolitan Australian people, moulded by the cultural, social and economic environment of the nation.

✓ **CHECK !**

Go back to the overview diagrams on pp. 36 and 57. If you are satisfied with your knowledge and understanding, tick off the sections that you have revised so far. If you are not satisfied, then revisit those sections and refer to the pages in the 'Need to know more?'

Section 11: *Mass participation in sport (Australia)*

Section overview

NEED TO KNOW MORE?

For further information on mass participation in Australia, see pp. 143–6 in *Advanced PE for OCR: A2.*

1 Introduction	☐
2 Popularity of colonial games	☐

Tick the box when you are satisfied with your level of knowledge and understanding for each topic within this section.

1 Introduction

The failure of the Australian team in the 1976 Olympic Games emphasised the need for federal involvement in sport.

- A master plan led to the establishment of the Australian Sports Commission (ASC).
- The aim of the ASC is to develop sports excellence and to increase community participation.
- The ASC has two 'delivery units' to ensure that sports participation is accessible for the whole population:

  1 The Australian Institute of Sport (AIS) trains elite teams and athletes.
  2 The Sport Development Group has the aim to increase sports participation through the More Active Australia and Active Australia policies.

HOT TIPS

Link the concept of mass participation to the work done in sport education and physical education in Australian schools.

The slogan Active Australia has been replaced by More Active Australia:

- The government invested AU$550 million in the scheme between 2000–04.

2 Popularity of colonial games

- Major games, with the exception of Australian football, remain as adoptions from the UK.
- The colonial elite established the hunt, golf and tennis clubs.

The hard-working 'new' Australians believed that true sportsmanship in competitive situations demanded moral effort and therefore sport was good for society.

- Cricket was the first sport to come to Australia from the UK, and the first game was played in Sydney around 1825.

- A home victory for Australia in the first test match in 1876 and success in England in 1882 created the 'Ashes' mythology.
- Cricket against the 'old masters' became a benchmark against which the progress of the young nation could be measured.

Rugby was also imported during colonial settlement:

- As in Britain, educational institutions were foremost in introducing rugby and Sydney University played the first game in 1863.
- Games on either side of the world were strictly amateur and catered for the middle classes.

Soccer did not transfer well to Australia:

- Soccer (the 'Pommie Game') was played initially by only British immigrants.
- With the influx of European setters after 1945, a new style of soccer involving control and skilful touches emerged.
- This continental style also introduced dissent toward officials, shirt pulling and foul tactics.

- Australians could not tolerate this approach and the labelled soccer an alien game.
- New European working-class immigrants remained in their ethnic groups and settled, forming 'ghetto cultures'. Their country of origin was reflected in the name of its soccer team. For example, Melbourne Croatia and St George Budapest. This stimulated racial rivalry and crowd violence.

Progress is now being made and the popularity of soccer is increasing:

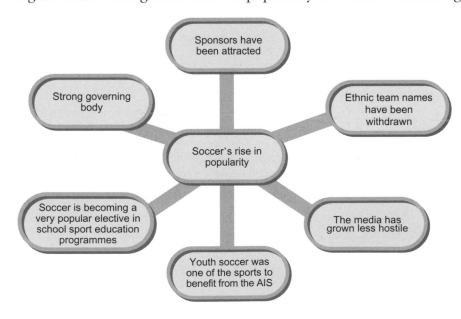

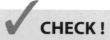 **CHECK !**

Go back to the overview diagrams on pp. 36 and 59. If you are satisfied with your knowledge and understanding, tick off the sections that you have revised so far. If you are not satisfied, then revisit those sections and refer to the pages in the 'Need to know more?'

Section 12: *Sport and the pursuit of excellence (Australia)*

Section overview

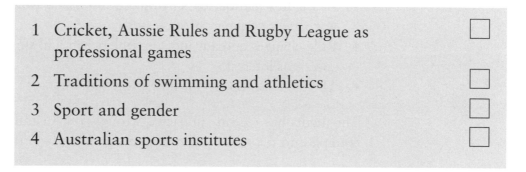

1 Cricket, Aussie Rules and Rugby League as professional games ☐

2 Traditions of swimming and athletics ☐

3 Sport and gender ☐

4 Australian sports institutes ☐

NEED TO KNOW MORE?

For further information on sport and the pursuit of excellence, see pp. 146–54 in *Advanced PE for OCR: A2.*

Tick the box when you are satisfied with your level of knowledge and understanding for each topic within this section.

1 Cricket, Aussie Rules and Rugby League as professional games

The development of cricket in the twentieth century has not been without controversy.

- The infamous 'bodyline' tour of 1932 – England's tactics were deemed unfair and both sporting and diplomatic relations became strained.
- The introduction of the 'World Series' in 1977 by Kerry Packer.

The focus of both Rugby League and Rugby Union remains in New South Wales and Queensland.

- Rugby League tends to be more popular.
- The breakaway movement to Rugby League came to Australia in 1907.
- This allowed professionalism (players could be paid for time spent away from work when playing).

During the 1970s, League attendances declined, necessitating major modifications.

- A five-team semi-final series, changes in scoring and the six-tackle rule were implemented to increase spectator appeal.
- The inaugural State of Origin match was played in 1980.
- The Rugby League game has salary-capped all players.
- Each professional 'club' has an 'academy'.

A major boost for Rugby Union was the inauguration of the World Cup in 1987.

- Success in this competition has increased sponsorship for the Australian Rugby Union and attracted greater television coverage.
- As the host nation, the Olympics (2000) and Rugby World Cup (2004) were great commercial successes.
- Rule changes and advances in athleticism and skilfulness have increased spectator interest.
- The game at top level is now professional.

The media has recently impacted strongly on Australian football. Revenue coming into the game has increased significantly in the last ten years.

- Games are played at strategic times throughout the weekend to attract large television audiences.
- Fixtures are organised in collusion with the television companies to ensure the most even distribution of 'star fixtures'.
- After a goal the referee will restart play only when a light on the scoreboard indicates that the commercial television break has ended.

A draft system operates to spread talent more evenly through the clubs.

2 Traditions of swimming and athletics

- Bathing was popular nationwide in colonial Australia.
- Swimming competitions were common for men.
- For women, exertion in sport was considered unfeminine.
- Australian women won medals at the Stockholm Olympics (1912) after special concessions were made allowing them to swim publicly.

A tradition of athletics is deeply rooted in Australian sports and social history.

- Australia has attended every Olympic games.
- In 1924 women entered the Olympic arena.

- Up to 2000, 75 per cent of Australia's gold medals in track and field have been won by women.
- There are great role models for both genders.

3 Sport and gender

'Frontier' and 'bush' attitudes of early colonialism laid down male domination.

- This led to serious discrimination towards women in sport.
- The concepts of feminism and fertility were thought to be threatened by participation.

During the 1950s and early 1960s, female champions emerged.

- Only after this was the male view challenged, and women adapted male styles and strategies in sport.
- Women were represented in horseracing, long-distance running, bodybuilding and, latterly, triathlon.

Today there is strong desire to address the issue of under-representation of women in sport.

- In 1995, the medical profession urged women to train and 'work out' like their male counterparts to achieve fitness.
- Sport education programmes are mixed whenever possible in schools.

The cultural factors that have impacted on sport are:

Bush culture	Reactive culture	Ambition	New image
Politics			Egalitarianism
	Colonialism		
Economy			Trends and fashion
Enlightenment	Climate	Global player	Unity and nationalism

4 Australian sports institutes

The National Network of Sports Institutions has a role to develop sports talent to the highest standard in Australia.

The Australian Institute of Sport (AIS) was opened in Canberra in 1981:

- It was funded by the Australian Sports Commission (ASC).

NEED TO KNOW MORE?

For further information on the development of excellence in Australian sport, compare the cricket pathway to excellence diagram, Fig. 2.53, p. 153, in *Advanced PE for OCR: A2* with the AFL pathway to excellence (Fig. 2.51, p. 149) which does not include involvement from the institute.

The AIS has been established in every state, for example:

- 1996 Northern Territory Institute of Sport (NTIS), Darwin.

State institutes and the AIS operate in parallel. There is no 'feeding' or relocating of athletes.

- Not all centres have onsite facilities.

Institutes are perceived as 'finishing schools'; however, they do not guarantee progress to higher level and can be bypassed.

Advantages of the institutes include:

- sports medicine services
- access to coaching
- financial subsidies
- education: Athletes Career Education (ACE) and/or vocational support
- national and international opportunities.

The system is closely monitored and administered by the National Elite Sports Council.

 CHECK !

Go back to the overview diagrams on pp. 36 and 61. If you are satisfied with your knowledge and understanding, tick off the sections that you have revised so far. If you are not satisfied, then revisit those sections and refer to the pages in the 'Need to know more?'

Section 13: *Outdoor education and outdoor recreation (Australia)*

Section overview

NEED TO KNOW MORE?

For further information on outdoor education and outdoor recreation, see pp. 154–7 in *Advanced PE for OCR: A2*.

1 Introduction	☐
2 The organisation of national and regional parks	☐
3 The role of outdoor education	☐

Tick the box when you are satisfied with your level of knowledge and understanding for each topic within this section.

1 Introduction

The interior of Australia has vast areas of genuine wilderness which provides opportunity for 'frontier experiences' outdoors. The 'beach culture', with traditions of swimming, surfing and lifesaving clubs, is the focus of a significant fitness cult.

2 The organisation of national and regional parks

- The federal government is promoting international tourism on a large scale.
- There are more than 500 national parks in Australia; for example, Uluru Park in central northern territory

3 The role of outdoor education

Outdoor education has a significant role in Australian schools and use of the natural environment is maximised.

- Primary schools offer outdoor adventure activities as part of a balanced physical education programme.
- Each state offers a Youth Development Programme.
- The Duke of Edinburgh Award scheme operates as a 'stand-alone' elective.

Skiing

- Victoria state inter-schools skiing championships take place at Camp Big Foot on Mount Buller.
- A non-elitist participation ethic is central to the mission of this state government subsidised enterprise.
- Over 4000 primary and secondary pupils and teachers attend this annual event and all categories of skiing are experienced.

Outward Bound

- The Outward Bound Trust also facilitates adventure opportunities.
- The trust, based on the UK model, has existed in Australia since the 1960s.
- There is an Outward Bound School at Tharwa in Australia's capital territories.

School initiatives

- Outdoor adventure packages are planned individually by enterprising teachers.
- Schools travel overseas for adventure experiences; for example, to Nepal and the South Island peaks of New Zealand.

Outdoor education as an examination subject

- During Years 11 and 12, outdoor education can be taken as a High School Certificate (HSC). The subject has a large theoretical input but involves practical assessment in a number of options.
- It is a popular examination elective and the subject is given high status.

Residential experiences

- The character-building concept relating to the outdoors pioneered by British public schools has continued in Australian independent schools.
- Timbertop is an upland forested adventure centre belonging to Geelong Grammar School for the purpose of residential experiences.
- The Alpine School is the Victoria State schools equivalent.
- In this venue courses in outdoor leadership and skills are delivered.
- The centre has a transient Year 9 population, as students are resident for ten weeks or one term.

HOT TIPS

A synoptic question will focus on a direct comparison between one country of study and the UK. However, synoptic marks will be awarded for relevant links to any country included in the comparative syllabus.

 CHECK !

Go back to the overview diagrams on pp. 1, 36 and 64. If you are satisfied with your knowledge and understanding, tick off the sections that you have revised so far. If you are not satisfied, then revisit those sections and refer to the pages in the 'Need to know more?'

Exam practice

1 Describe the crisis that has emerged within physical education in US schools and explain how the problem is being addressed. **(4 marks)**

2 By referring to short-term benefits and wider cultural attractions, explain why a US high school player would accept a sports scholarship. **(7 marks)**

3 Explain why the status of physical education has increased in French schools during the last ten years. **(4 marks)**

4 (a) In 2003, 50 per cent of French people claimed to participate in sport.
  (b) Explain how this target has been achieved in France. Describe the strategies that exist in the UK to promote mass participation in sport. **(13 knowledge marks)**

NEED TO KNOW MORE?

For further information on knowledge marks, see pp. 166 and 173.

5 In Australia the former colonial games are popular, but soccer has experienced problems. Outline the problems of an ethnic nature encountered by soccer in Australia and identify the measures taken to overcome them. **(5 marks)**

6 Explain why Aussie Rules football is known as a 'new game' and describe how it has developed into a game of the people. **(3 marks)**

7 What cultural factors make outdoor education an important subject in Australian schools? **(4 marks)**

Now go to p. 172 to check your answers.

Chapter 3 **Biomechanics**

Chapter overview

1 Linear motion ☐

2 Force ☐

3 Projectile motion ☐

4 Angular motion ☐

Tick the box when you are satisfied with your level of knowledge and understanding for each section within this chapter.

Section 1: *Linear motion*

Section overview

NEED TO KNOW MORE?

For further information on linear motion, see pp. 158–71 in *Advanced PE for OCR: A2*.

1 Introduction ☐

2 Newton's Laws of Motion ☐

3 Measurements used in linear motion ☐

4 Scalar quantity v. vector quantity ☐

5 Graphs of motion ☐

Tick the box when you are satisfied with your level of knowledge and understanding for each topic within this section.

1 Introduction

Linear motion

KEY WORDS

Linear motion

mass

- is when a body moves in a straight or curved line with all its parts moving the same distance, in the same direction, and at the same speed
- occurs when an 'on centre' force (one that passes through the **centre of mass**) is applied to a body.

Example: a tobogganist moving in a straight line.

2 Newton's Laws of Motion

Newton's First Law of Motion

KEY WORDS

Newton's First Law of Motion

Inertia

Newton's Second Law of Motion

Acceleration

- 'A body continues in a state of rest or uniform velocity unless acted upon by an external force.'
- Newton's first law is often referred to as the 'Law of **Inertia**'.
- The inertia of a stationary object is its resistance to accelerate.
- The inertia of a moving object is its resistance to accelerate, decelerate or change direction.

Example: a football will remain at rest until a player applies a force by kicking it.

Example: a runner will move with constant velocity if the horizontal forces are balanced, for example when friction and air resistance are equal and opposite.

Newton's Second Law of Motion

NEED TO KNOW MORE?

For further information on impulse, see pp. 80–1 of this book.

- 'When a force acts on an object, the rate of change of momentum experienced by the object is proportional to the size of the force and takes place in the direction in which the force acts.'
- Newton's second law is often referred to as the 'Law of Momentum' or the 'Law of **Acceleration**'.
- It can be expressed as: Force = mass × acceleration ($F = ma$).
- The acceleration of an object is proportional to the size of the force acting upon it and will take place in the same direction as the force.

Example: the harder a football is kicked, the greater its acceleration and the further it will travel in the direction that the force is applied.

- The principle of 'impulse' is also closely related to Newton's second law.

KEY WORDS

Newton's Third Law of Motion

Action force

Reaction force

Newton's Third Law of Motion

- 'For every force that is exerted by one body on another there is an equal and opposite force exerted by the second body on the first.'
- Newton's third law is often referred to as the 'Law of Reaction'.
- **Action force** is force exerted by the athlete.
- **Reaction force** is the equal and opposite force exerted by another object on the athlete as a result of the action force.

NEED TO KNOW MORE?

For further information on reaction force, see p. 76 of this book.

Example: when a football is kicked, the action force is the force exerted by the foot on to the ball and the reaction force is the equal and opposite force exerted by the ball on to the foot as a result of the kick.

3 Measurements used in linear motion

Mass

This is the 'quantity of matter' of a body.

- An athlete's mass is made from muscle, bone, fat, tissue and fluid.
- The more matter from which a body is made, the greater is its mass.
- Mass is measured in kilograms (kg).
- Mass is a scalar quantity.

Inertia

- This is the resistance of a body to change its state of rest or motion.
- The inertia of a body depends on its mass.
- The bigger the mass, the larger the inertia of a body and the greater the force must be to change its state of motion.

Example: a rugby player with a big mass will require a big force to get them moving, but once moving it will be very difficult for them to stop due to their large inertia.

Distance v. displacement

Distance

- **Distance** is how far a body has travelled to get from one position to another.
- It is measured in metres (m).
- It is a **scalar quantity**.

Displacement

- **Displacement** is the shortest straight-line route between two positions in a stated direction.
- It is measured in metres (m).
- It is a **vector quantity**, so it is important to give a direction when describing displacement.

Example: an athlete who completes one lap of an athletics track will have covered a distance of 400m but their displacement will be 0m.

Speed v. velocity

Speed

- **Speed** is the rate of change of distance.
- Speed = distance/time.
- It is measured in metres per second (ms^{-1}).
- It is a scalar quantity.

Velocity
- **Velocity** is the rate of change of displacement.
- Velocity = displacement/time.
- It is measured in metres per second (ms^{-1}).
- It is a vector quantity.

Example: an athlete who completes one lap of an athletics track in 60 seconds would have had an average speed of $400/60 = 6.7ms^{-1}$, whereas their average velocity would have been $0/60 = 0ms^{-1}$.

Acceleration

- **Acceleration** is the rate of change of velocity.
- Acceleration = change in velocity/time or $a = v–u/t$ where v represents final velocity and u represents initial velocity.
- It is measured in metres per second per second (ms^{-2}).
- It is a vector quantity and this is why **deceleration** is often referred to as negative acceleration and a minus sign is found in front of its value.
- **Zero acceleration** occurs when all the forces acting on a body are balanced (resultant force = 0) and the body is either at rest or moving with constant velocity.
- For an acceleration to occur an unbalanced force needs to be applied to a body.

Example: a sprinter who reaches a velocity of $6ms^{-1}$ two seconds after a sprint start will have an average acceleration of $v–u/t = 6–0/2 = 3ms^{-2}$.

Momentum

- **Momentum** is the quantity of motion possessed by a body.
- It is a product of the mass and velocity of a body.
- Momentum = mass × velocity.
- It is measured in kilogram metres per second ($kgms^{-1}$).
- It is a vector quantity.

Example: a rugby player with a mass of 90kg who is running with a velocity of $8ms^{-1}$ will have a momentum of $90 × 8 = 720kgms^{-1}$.

4 Scalar quantity v. vector quantity
Scalar quantity

- This is an indication of magnitude (size) only.
- Measurements include mass, inertia, distance and speed.

Vector quantity

- This gives an indication of magnitude (size) and direction.
- Measurements include displacement, velocity, acceleration, momentum and force.

5 Graphs of motion

Distance/time graphs

- These indicate the distance travelled by an object after a certain time.
- The **gradient** of a distance/time curve represents the speed of an object.

For distance/time graphs:

horizontal line	= no motion	(A–B)
positive curve	= acceleration	(B–C)
regular diagonal line	= constant speed	(C–D)
negative curve	= deceleration	(D–E)

gradient of curve $= \dfrac{distance}{time} = speed$

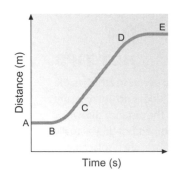

Fig. 3.01 A typical distance/time curve for a hockey pass between two players on Astroturf (assuming the friction between the ball and the surface is negligible).

For distance/time curves:

(A–B) horizontal line	= no motion as ball is at rest before being hit
(B–C) positive curve	= acceleration of the ball as it is hit
(C–D) regular diagonal line	= constant speed of the ball as it travels between players
(D–E) negative curve	= deceleration of the ball as it is controlled

Velocity/time graphs

- These indicate the velocity of an object after a certain time.
- The area underneath a velocity/time graph represents the distance travelled by an object.
- The gradient of a velocity/time graph represents the acceleration of an object.

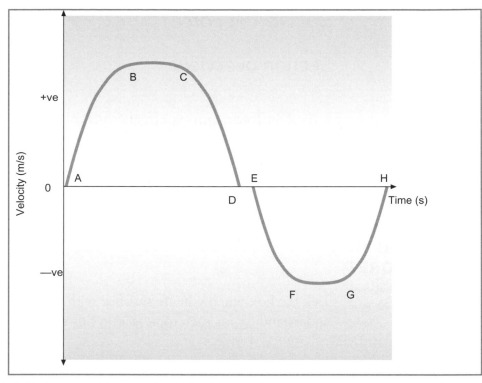

Fig. 3.02 A velocity/time graph for a hockey pass between two players on Astroturf (assuming the friction between the ball and the surface is negligible) in which the ball is stopped momentarily before being passed straight back to the original passer.

For velocity/time curves:

(A–B) positive curve	= acceleration of the ball while in contact with the stick
(B–C) horizontal line	= constant velocity of the ball between the players
(C–D) negative curve	= deceleration of the ball when it is controlled
(D–E) horizontal line	= stationary ball when it is stopped momentarily
(E–H) curve below the × axis	= change in direction of the ball as it is passed back

HOT TIPS

To gain maximum marks for a velocity/time graph:

• Always plot velocity on the y axis and time on the × axis.
• Always label the axes and identify the units.
• Plot the points accurately and draw a curve of best fit.

HOT TIPS

Remember that velocity is a vector quantity and that direction matters.

HOT TIPS

The slope of a graph at a particular moment in time is the gradient. It is calculated as: Gradient of graph = changes in y axis/changes in × axis.

 **CHECK !**

Go back to the overview diagrams on p. 68. If you are satisfied with your knowledge and understanding, tick off the sections that you have revised so far. If you are not satisfied, then revisit those sections and refer to the pages in the 'Need to know more?'

Section 2: *Force*

Section overview

1 Net force and its effects	☐
2 Types of force acting on a sports performer	☐
3 Free body diagrams	☐
4 Impulse	☐
5 Work and power	☐

NEED TO KNOW MORE?

For further information on force, see pp. 172–87 in *Advanced PE for OCR: A2*.

Tick the box when you are satisfied with your level of knowledge and understanding for each topic within this section.

1 Net force and its effects

KEY WORDS

Force

Net force

Internal force

External force

Force:

- is a pull or a push that alters, or tends to alter, the state of motion of a body
- is a vector (so has both size and direction)
- can be calculated using $F = ma$ (Newton's second law)
- is measured in Newtons.

Net force:

- is the overall force acting on a body when all the individual forces have been considered
- is the sum of all forces acting on a body
- is also termed the 'resultant force'.

NEED TO KNOW MORE?

For further information on force, see p. 45 in *Advanced PE for OCR: AS*.

Internal force:

- is a force generated through the contraction of skeletal muscle.

External force:

- is a force that comes from outside the body; for example, weight, reaction, friction and air resistance.

The effects of a net force:

- cause a resting body to move (accelerate)
- cause a moving body to accelerate, decelerate or change direction
- change an object's shape.

When describing a force, three things need to be considered:

- the point of application of the force
- the size of the force
- the direction of the force.

Whenever an arrow is drawn to represent a force, three important things need to be considered to gain marks in an examination question:

- The point of application of the force – shown by the point at which the arrow begins.
- The size of the force – shown by the length of the arrow. The larger the force, the longer the arrow.
- The direction of the force – shown by the direction of the arrow.

Balanced forces

- Balanced forces occur when two or more forces on a body are equal in size but opposite in direction – they cancel each other out.
- This means that the net force acting on the body is zero.
- The body will either remain stationary or move with constant velocity (Newton's first law).

Unbalanced forces

- Unbalanced forces occur when a force acting in one direction on a body is greater in size than a force acting in the opposite direction.
- This means that there will be a net force acting on the body.
- The body will accelerate in the direction of the net force (Newton's second law).

2 Types of force acting on a sports performer

The external forces that act on a sports performer can be divided into vertical and horizontal forces. Forces acting on a body in water are given different names to those acting on the ground.

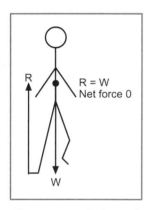

Fig. 3.03 In a balanced and stationary position the two forces acting on a body are weight and reaction. These forces are equal in size but opposite in direction. The net force = 0 and there is no change in motion.

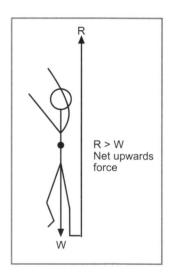

Fig. 3.04 The upward reaction force of a high jumper is greater than the downward weight force. There is a net force in the upward direction and the high jumper is able to leave the ground.

	Ground	Water
Vertical	**Weight** and **reaction force**	**Weight** and **buoyancy**
Horizontal	**Friction force** and **air resistance**	**Forward force** or **thrust** and **drag** (or **fluid friction**)

Vertical forces

Weight

- Weight is the **gravitational force** that the earth exerts on a body.
- $W = m \times g$ where m = mass of the body and g = acceleration due to gravity (usually assumed to be 10ms^{-2}).
- Weight acts downwards from the centre of mass of a body.
- It is measured in Newtons.

HOT TIPS

W = mg is a simple re-arrangement of Newton's second law (F = ma). The force is weight, the mass stays the same and the acceleration is g (gravitational acceleration).

Gravitational force

- **Gravitational force** is the force that attracts a body to the centre of the Earth.

Mass and weight are not the same. Mass is the quantity of matter of an object and is measured in kilograms (kg). The mass of an athlete stays the same, but the weight of an athlete can change depending on gravity. An athlete will have less weight at the equator than at the North Pole even though his mass will stay the same, as gravity is less effective at the equator.

HOT TIPS

When a sprinter pushes downwards and backwards on the ground at the start of a race, the ground provides an equal and opposite reaction force upwards and forwards on the sprinter. This is sometimes called the ground reaction force.

Reaction force

- Reaction force comes about as a result of Newton's Third Law of Motion.
- It is the equal and opposite force exerted by a body in response to a force exerted on it by another body.
- It will always be present whenever two bodies are in contact with each other.
- It is measured in Newtons.

HOT TIPS

The normal reaction is the vertical component of the ground reaction force and acts perpendicular (at right angles) to the ground. The horizontal component of the ground reaction force is friction (parallel to the surface).

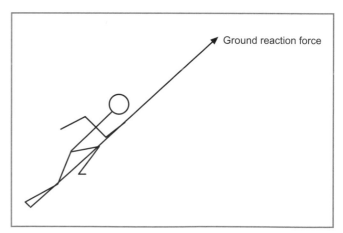

Ground reaction force

Fig. 3.05 The ground reaction force acting on a sprinter at the start of a race.

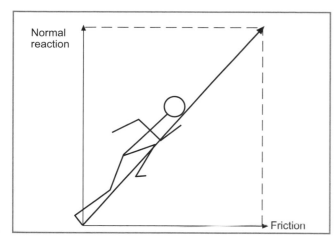

Fig. 3.06 The vertical and horizontal component forces of the ground reaction force acting on a sprinter at the start of a race.

Horizontal forces

Friction force

- Friction force occurs whenever one object moves or tends to move across the surface of another.
- It will oppose the movement or tendency to move.
- It will act parallel to the surfaces in contact.
- It depends on the degree of roughness between the two contact surfaces; the rougher the surface, the greater the frictional force.
- It depends on the normal reaction between the two contact surfaces; the larger the normal reaction, the greater the frictional force.

Air resistance/fluid friction/drag

This is the force acting in the opposite direction to the motion of a body travelling through the air or water. It depends on:

- the velocity of the object (as velocity doubles, air resistance will quadruple)
- the forward cross-sectional area of the object (the bigger the forward cross-sectional area, the greater the air resistance)
- the shape of the object (the less streamlined the object, the greater the air resistance)
- the surface characteristics of the object (the rougher the surfaces, the greater the air resistance)
- the density of the air/water through which the object moves (the denser the air, the greater the air resistance).

Streamlining is an attempt to create a more aerodynamic shape:

- by creating a smoother air/fluid flow around an object
- by reducing the air resistance/drag behind it.

Example: the smooth, 'teardrop' shaped helmets used by cyclists and speed skiers.

Swimmers:

- shave body hair
- wear swimming caps and 'shark suits'
- swim underwater for as long as possible in some events
- use a dolphin action wherever possible.

Cyclists/skiers:

- use tucked body positions
- wear lycra clothing
- wear streamlined helmets.

3 Free body diagrams

Free body diagrams

These are clearly labelled sketches used to show all the forces acting on an object at a particular moment in time.

The most common forces shown on a free body diagram are:

HOT TIPS

For the purposes of the examination, 'stick men' are used to show the forces acting on the human body at a particular moment in time, as illustrated in Figure 3.07.

- weight
- reaction
- friction
- air resistance.

(Sometimes Bernoulli and Magnus effects are shown in projectile free body diagrams)

As force is a vector, it can be represented by a straight arrow which can show:

HOT TIPS

When sketching free body diagrams, draw a direction of motion arrow. In addition, make a comment about the net force in the vertical direction and the net force in the horizontal direction below or beside your sketch in order to clarify to the examiner the relative sizes of the forces acting.

- point of application of the force (beginning of the line)
- direction of force (arrow at the end of the line)
- size of the force (length of the line).

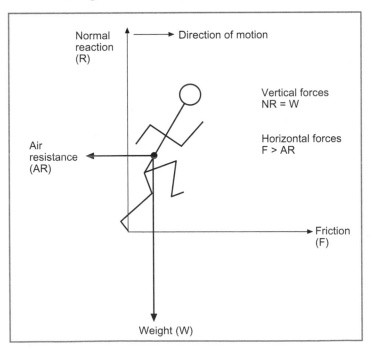

Fig. 3.07 The forces acting on a runner who is accelerating.

	1 **Weight (W)**	2 **Reaction (R)**	3 **Friction (F)**	4 **Air resistance (AR)**
Origin of arrow	From the centre of mass	From the point(s) of contact of two bodies	From the point(s) of contact of two bodies	From the centre of mass
Direction of arrow	Vertically downward	Perpendicular to the surface of contact, usually vertically upward. (For the purposes of A2 biomechanics, it is easier to consider the **normal reaction** force that is drawn at right angles to the ground)	Opposite to the direction of the intended slipping action between the two bodies. This is usually in the same direction as motion	Opposite to the direction of motion of the body
Length of arrow	Dependent on the mass. Bodies with larger masses will have longer weight arrows than bodies with smaller masses	Dependent on the resulting motion and the length of the weight arrow. As a result of Newton's first and second laws: If $R = W$, net force = 0. If $R > W$, the body will accelerate upwards. If $R < W$, the body will accelerate downwards.	Dependent on the resulting motion and the length of the air resistance arrow	Dependent on the resulting motion and the length of the friction arrow. As a result of Newton's first and second laws: If $F = AR$, net force = 0. If $F > AR$, the body will accelerate. If $F < AR$, the body will decelerate.
Label	W	R	F	AR

Fig. 3.08 This table summarises the importance of the origin, direction and length of the arrows used to represent weight, reaction, friction and air resistance.

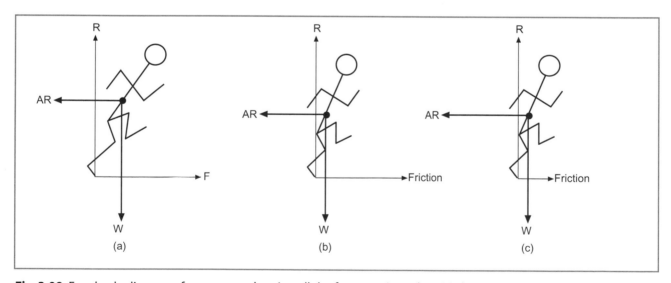

Fig. 3.09 Free body diagrams for a runner showing all the forces acting when (a) the runner is accelerating; (b) the runner is moving with constant velocity; (c) the runner is decelerating.

HOT TIPS

To help you gain maximum marks, it is important that you practise drawing free body diagrams.

(a) Vertical forces: $W = R$, net force = 0, no acceleration
Horizontal forces: $F > AR$, forward acceleration

(b) Vertical forces: $W = R$, net force = 0, no acceleration
Horizontal forces: $F = AR$, net force = 0, no acceleration
Runner continues with constant velocity

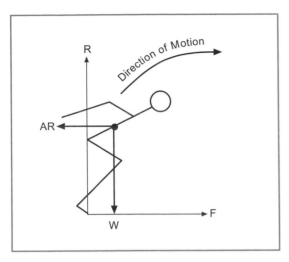

Fig. 3.10 A free body diagram showing the forces acting on a swimmer on the blocks during take off.

KEY WORDS

Impulse

(c) Vertical forces: W = R, net force = 0, no acceleration
Horizontal forces: F < AR, deceleration

Vertical forces: W < R, upward acceleration
Horizontal forces: F > AR, forward acceleration

4 Impulse

- Impulse is the term given to the product of the force and the time for which it acts.
- Impulse = Force × Time, I = Ft.
- Units are Newton seconds (Ns).
- Impulse = Change in momentum, or Ft = mv – mu.

Athletes can increase impulse in two ways:

- increasing the amount of force applied
- increasing the time that the force is applied.

For example:

- Elite shot/discus throwers use a one and three-quarter turn.
- High jumpers lean backwards as they plant their foot at take off.
- Games players use a bigger follow through when striking a ball.

Effect of the follow through when striking a ball:

- Increases the *time* that the force is applied to the ball,
- which increases the *impulse* of force applied to the ball.
- This increases the *outgoing momentum* of the ball,
- which leads to an increase in the *outgoing velocity* of the ball,
- therefore increasing the *distance* the ball may travel.
- It also gives the player greater control over the *direction* through which the ball moves.

Knowledge of impulse can also be used to slow down or stop a body/object safely. By increasing the time it takes to stop an object, the force applied to that body decreases. For example:

- Ski jumpers/gymnasts bend their knees on landing.
- Crash mats prevent injury to high jumpers and pole vaulters.
- Cricketers let their hands/body 'ride' with the ball when catching.

Graphical representation of impulse:

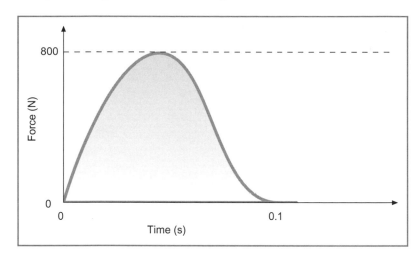

Fig. 3.11 A force/time graph for a tennis ball being hit during a forehand drive.

The area underneath the force/time curve represents the impulse of force imparted to the ball during impact.

Impulse = area under force/time curve $= \dfrac{1}{2} \times 800 \times 0.1 = 40\text{Ns}$

5 Work and power

Work is done when a force is applied to a body to move it over a certain distance.

- Work done = force × distance moved, (W = Fd)
- Units of measurement for work are joules (J) or Newton metres (Nm).

Power is important in all sports as it is the ability to perform work at high speeds.

- Power $= \dfrac{\text{work done}}{\text{time taken}}$

    $= \dfrac{\text{force} \times \text{distance}}{\text{time taken}}$

    $= \dfrac{\text{force}}{\text{velocity}}.$

- Power is the rate at which work is done.
- Units of measurement for power are watts (w).

For example, if an athlete exerts a force of 750N in lifting a weight 2 metres above the floor, then:

Work done = Fd
= 750×2
= 1500 joules

If the athlete performed this in 1.5 seconds, then:

Power = $\dfrac{\text{work done}}{\text{time taken}}$

= $\dfrac{1500}{1.5}$

= 1000w

 CHECK !

Go back to the overview diagrams on pp. 68 and 74. If you are satisfied with your knowledge and understanding, tick off the sections that you have revised so far. If you are not satisfied, then revisit those sections and refer to the pages in the 'Need to know more?'

Section 3: *Projectile motion*

1 Introduction ☐
2 The release of projectiles ☐
3 Projectiles and forces in flight ☐
4 Projectiles and free body diagrams ☐
5 Projectiles and parallelogram of forces ☐
6 Projectiles and lift (Bernoulli Principle) ☐
7 Projectiles and spin (Magnus effect) ☐
8 Effect of spin on bouncing ☐

Tick the box when you are satisfied with your level of knowledge and understanding for each topic within this section.

1 Introduction

- Projectile motion occurs when a human body or object is launched into the air that is subject only to forces of weight and air resistance (including the effects of lift or spin).
- Whenever athletes break contact with the ground or objects are released, they become **projectiles.**

Examples include long jumpers and high jumpers in athletics, ski jumpers, gymnasts and divers or balls in flight, shuttlecocks and javelins.

2 The release of projectiles

The horizontal distance that a projectile travels during its flight depends on a combination of factors.

HOT TIPS

In some sports, such as the high jump, it is not just horizontal distance that is needed but also maximum vertical distance. An athlete must manipulate his or her angle of release depending on each situation.

Angle of release

To achieve maximum horizontal distance, the optimal **angle of release** for a projectile is:

- 45 degrees if the release height is equal to the landing height; for example, a footballer executing a lofted goal kick
- less than 45 degrees if the release height is greater than the landing height; for example, in the shot put
- more than 45 degrees if the release height is less than the landing height; for example, a bunker shot in golf.

KEY WORDS

Angle of release

Velocity of release

Height of release

Velocity of release

The greater the **velocity of release**, the greater the horizontal distance achieved by a projectile; for example, a long jumper tries to achieve maximum speed at take off.

HOT TIPS

Lift forces and spin will also affect the distance travelled by a projectile. This is explained on pages 86–89 of this book.

Height of release

As the **height of release** increases, horizontal distance travelled is increased for a given angle and velocity of release.

KEY WORDS

Parabolic/symmetrical flight path

Non-parabolic/asymmetrical flight path

3 Projectiles and forces in flight

- Projectiles are acted upon by two forces: weight and air resistance.
- A **parabolic/symmetrical flight path** occurs when the weight of the projectile is the dominant force and air resistance is negligible; for example, a shot in flight.
- A **non-parabolic/asymmetrical flight path** occurs when the air resistance of a projectile becomes more dominant when compared to its weight; for example, when a shuttlecock is struck hard.
- Fast-moving objects with a large frontal cross-sectional area and a rough outer surface will follow a non-parabolic flight path.
- Lift (Bernoulli Principle) and spin (Magnus effect) provide extra forces acting on a projectile during flight.

NEED TO KNOW MORE?

The Bernoulli Principle and Magnus effect are explained further on pp. 86–9 of this book.

4 Projectiles and free body diagrams

- The forces acting on a projectile in flight can be represented using a free body diagram.
- The origin, direction and length of the arrow used to represent weight and air resistance (and Bernoulli/Magnus if appropriate) are still important.
- When drawing free body diagrams of projectiles, always remember to include the direction of motion arrow.
- Air resistance is always opposite the direction of motion and, for, the purposes of the examination, acts from the centre of mass of the projectile.
- Weight always acts downwards from the centre of mass of the projectile.

Example: for the shot put the weight force will be considerably larger than the air resistance force because it is heavy. Air resistance is relatively small as the shot travels slowly, it has a small frontal cross-sectional area relative to its mass and it has a reasonably smooth outer surface. Air resistance also changes direction during flight. A free body diagram for the shot put during flight is shown in Figure 3.12.

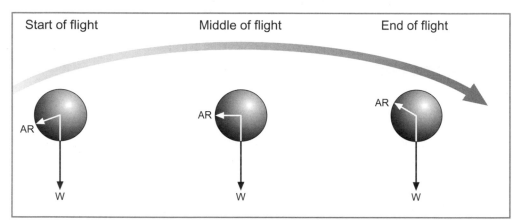

Fig. 3.12 Free body diagrams to show the forces acting on a shot put during various stages of flight.

HOT TIPS

The flight path of the shot is parabolic throughout its flight as weight is dominant and air resistance is negligible throughout. For the well-struck shuttle, the flight path is non-parabolic at the start but by the end it has become more parabolic as air resistance has reduced significantly.

Example: for the well-struck shuttle, the weight force is considerably smaller than the air resistance force because it is light. Air is resistance relatively large at the start of its flight as it is travelling quickly and it has a rough outer surface. The effect of air resistance reduces during flight as it slows down quickly because of its large air resistance. A free body diagram for the shuttle during flight is shown in Figure 3.13.

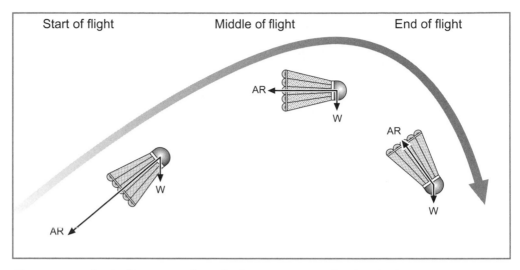

Fig. 3.13 Free body diagram to show the forces acting on the shuttle during various stages of flight.

5 Projectiles and parallelogram of forces

- The parallelogram of forces enables us to work out the **resultant force** acting on an object.
- The resultant force represents the sum of all the forces acting on a body.
- The direction and length of the resultant force is determined by sketching a parallelogram of forces.
- To ensure the correct direction of a resultant force, use the component force arrows (usually weight and air resistance) as two sides of a parallelogram:
  - Construct the missing sides to complete the parallelogram.
  - Draw in a diagonal line from the origin of the forces to the opposite corner of the parallelogram.
  - This diagonal arrow represents the resultant force.
- The resultant force shows the acceleration of a body and the direction in which it takes place.

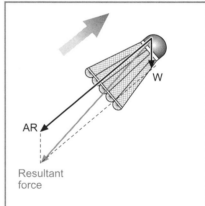

Fig. 3.14 Using the parallelogram of forces to show the resultant force acting on a shuttle at the start of flight. The resultant force for the shuttle is in almost the same direction as air resistance, meaning that the flight path of the shuttle is non-parabolic.

6 Projectiles and lift (Bernoulli Principle)

• Lift will enable a projectile to stay in the air longer and achieve a greater horizontal distance.
• The effect of lift is based on the **Bernoulli Principle**.
• It occurs when a projectile takes on the shape of an aerofoil/wing.
• The 'angle of attack' will affect the size of the lift force.
• Air travels further and therefore faster over the top of the projectile.
• Faster air causes low pressure above the projectile and therefore a pressure gradient from high to low pressure is created.
• This causes a lift force to act on the projectile.
• This effect is used in throwing the javelin and discus, and in ski jumping.
• This effect is used in reverse by Formula 1 racing cars using spoilers to create 'downforce' in order to generate more friction between the tyres and road surface.

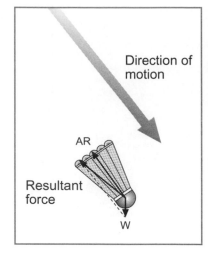

Fig. 3.15 Using the parallelogram of forces to show the resultant force acting on a shuttle during the final part of flight. The resultant force for the shuttle is now closer to the direction of weight meaning its flight has become more parabolic.

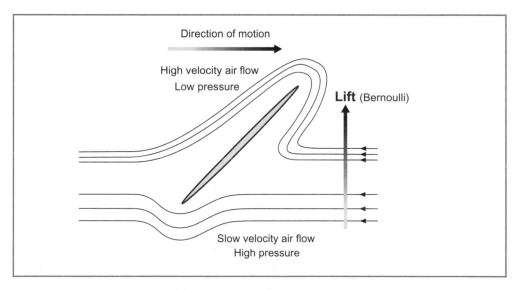

Fig. 3.16 The airflow patterns created by a javelin flying at the correct angle of attack produce a lift force that increases the horizontal distance covered.

KEY WORDS

Magnus effect

HOT TIPS

For a right-handed golfer, a hook describes the ball swerving to the left and a slice describes the ball swerving to the right.

7 Projectiles and spin (Magnus effect)

- The effects of spin on the flight path of an object are usually concerned with balls in games such as tennis, table tennis, football, golf and cricket.

The principle causing this deviation in flight path is the **Magnus effect**.

- Spin is created by the application of an 'off-centre' force, where the force applied does not pass through the centre of mass of the object.
- The three main types of spin are top spin, back spin and side spin:
  - Top spin makes the ball dip thereby making its flight path shorter and non-parabolic.
  - Back spin makes the ball float thereby making its flight path longer and non-parabolic.
  - Side spin makes the ball swerve.

Top spin	Back spin
View from side	View from side
Ball dips	Ball floats
Decreases distance travelled	Increases distance travelled

Hook	Slice
View from top	View from top
Ball deviates left	Ball deviates right

Fig. 3.17 The deviations in flight path caused by imparting spin to a projectile at the point of release.

To ensure you score maximum marks when sketching diagrams to show the deviation in flight path caused by spin, remember to follow these stages:

- Label your sketch with the type of spin being shown.
- State whether the sketch is viewed from the side (top/back spin) or from above (side spin).
- Show the direction of motion.
- Show the direction of spin.
- Sketch both the spinning and non-spinning flight path so that the deviation is obvious.
- State the effect of the spin.

For top spin:

- Air flowing over the top of the ball will be opposite the direction of spin and will slow down due to the friction between the air and the surface of the ball.
- Air flowing underneath the ball will be in the same direction as the spin and will speed up.
- Therefore air will flow faster underneath the ball than over the top.
- Therefore low pressure will be created underneath the ball and high pressure on top of the ball.
- This causes the ball to deviate towards the area of low pressure.
- The ball dips and the flight path is shortened.

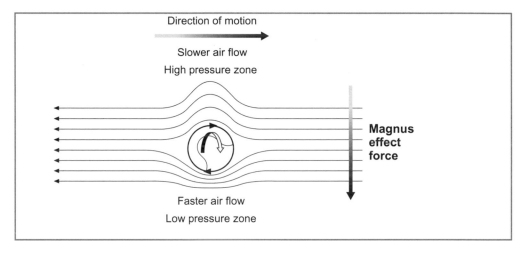

Fig. 3.18 Top spin: view from the side.

For back spin:

- Air flowing underneath the ball will be opposite the direction of spin and will slow down.
- Air flowing over the top of the ball will be in the same direction as the spin and will speed up.
- Therefore air will flow faster over the top of the ball than underneath.
- Therefore low pressure will be created over the top of the ball and high pressure underneath the ball.

- This causes the ball to deviate towards the area of low pressure.
- The ball floats and the flight path is lengthened.

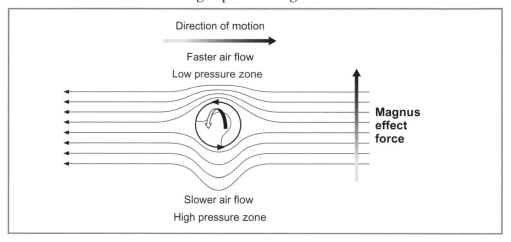

Fig. 3.19 Back spin: view from the side.

To ensure you score maximum marks when explaining the Magnus effect using airflow diagrams, remember to follow these stages:

- Label the type of spin to be sketched (top/back/side).
- Identify the best way to view the diagram (from the side/from above).
- Show the direction of motion.
- Draw the ball.
- Show the direction of spin.
- Show the direction of airflow using arrows on airflow lines (opposite the direction of motion).
- Airflow lines are narrower for faster flowing air/low pressure zones.
- Airflow lines are wider for slower flowing air/high pressure zones.
- State where airflow is fast and where it is slow.
- State where pressure is low and where it is high.
- Insert the overall Magnus effect arrow (perpendicular to the direction of motion).

8 The effect of spin on bouncing

Top spin:

- Friction will act in a forward direction.
- The ball will increase in speed on bouncing.
- The ball will shoot forward at a low angle from the ground.

Back spin:

- Friction will act in a backward direction.
- The ball will decrease in speed on bouncing.
- The ball will kick up at a large angle from the ground.

✔ **CHECK !**

Go back to the overview diagrams on pp. 68 and 82. If you are satisfied with your knowledge and understanding, tick off the sections that you have revised so far. If you are not satisfied, then revisit those sections and refer to the pages in the 'Need to know more?'

Section 4: *Angular motion*

Section overview

1 Introduction	☐
2 Centre of mass	☐
3 Levers	☐
4 Principle of moments	☐
5 Principle axes of rotation	☐
6 Measurements used in angular motion	☐
7 Angular analogues of Newton's Laws	☐
8 Moment of inertia	☐
9 Angular momentum	☐

NEED TO KNOW MORE?

For further information on angular motion, see pp. 42–52 in *Advanced PE for OCR: AS* and pp. 200–18 in *Advanced PE for OCR: A2*.

Tick the box when you are satisfied with your level of knowledge and understanding for each topic within this section.

1 Introduction

- **Angular motion** is when a body or part of a body moves in a circle or part of a circle about an axis of rotation.
- occurs when an 'off-centre' force (one that does not pass through the centre of mass) is applied to a body.

This happens when athletes are required to turn, spin, twist, somersault, swing or rotate. Other examples are when our limbs rotate about our joints as in knee flexion and extension.

HOT TIPS

General motion is a combination of linear and angular motion such as exhibited by 100m sprinters. They display linear motion as they move along the track, but their arms and legs exhibit angular motion.

2 Centre of mass

- **Centre of mass** is the point at which an object is balanced in all directions.

KEY WORDS

Angular motion

Centre of mass

- It is the point of a body where all of its mass could be considered to be concentrated.
- This is the point at which the weight of a body appears to act.
- Its position depends on the distribution of mass about a body and it can change as a result of a change in body shape (see Figure 3.20).
- Its position can lie outside the body (see Figure 3.21).
- When the centre of mass lies within the base of support of a body, then the body is balanced (stable equilibrium).
- When the centre of mass lies outside the base of support of a body, the body is unbalanced (unstable equilibrium) as the body's weight acts as a moment of force about the edge of the base of support (axis of rotation).
- By widening the base of support of a body and lowering its centre of mass, the **stability** of a body is increased; for example, rugby players will widen their stance and bend their knees to increase their stability when making a head-on tackle.

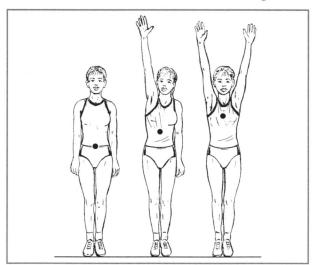

Fig. 3.20 A change in body position causes a shift in the position of the centre of mass. The amount of shift is dependent on the mass of the body parts moved and the distance they have moved.

- It is the centre of mass of a projectile that follows a predetermined flight path if no outside forces act upon it. If an athlete takes off with a high centre of mass (arms and one knee up), then they can lower their centre of mass (lowering one arm and knee) during flight, thereby increasing the height that can be reached. Basketball players and goalkeepers are examples of athletes that do this to reach high balls.
- If a force is applied through the centre of mass (on centre/direct force) of a body, the result is linear motion.
- If a force is applied outside the centre of mass (off centre/eccentric force) of a body, the result will include some angular motion (see Figure 3.22).

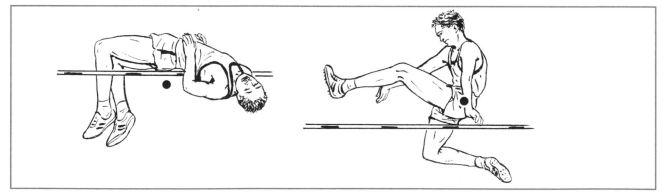

Fig. 3.21 The 'bridge' shape adopted by a high jumper performing a Fosbury flop means that the centre of mass of the high jumper can pass underneath the bar while the high jumper can pass over it.

KEY WORDS

Lever

Fulcrum

Load

Effort

First class lever

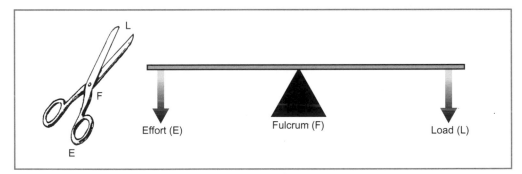

Fig. 3.22 When performing a back somersault, the trampolinist will lean back slightly at take off so that the reaction force passes outside the centre of mass to ensure that angular motion is created.

3 Levers

A **lever** is a rigid structure, hinged at one point (**fulcrum**) and to which two forces are applied at two other points (**load** and **effort**).

In the human body:

- a lever is a bone
- a fulcrum/pivot is a joint
- the effort is the force exerted by the muscle on the bone
- the load is the force that acts as a resistance to the lever system and is made up of the weight of the limb/body plus any other object to be moved.

Classification of levers

First class lever system

- The fulcrum is located between the load and the effort.
- An example is found during extension of the neck.
- The fulcrum is the joint between the atlas and the cranium (atlanto-occipital).
- The load is the weight of the head that causes the head to tilt/rotate forwards.
- The effort is the force applied by the trapezius muscle as it contracts to pull/rotate the head backwards.
- The lever is the cranium/occipital bone.

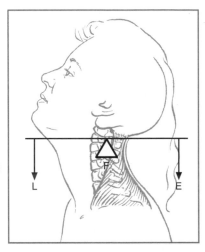

Fig. 3.23 Extension of the neck is a **first class lever** system.

Fig. 3.24 The fulcrum is located between the load and the effort in a first class lever system.

Second class lever system

- The load is located between the fulcrum and the effort.
- An example is found in the toe joints when an athlete stands on tiptoe.
- The fulcrum is the joint between the metatarsals and the phalanges.

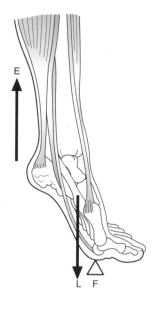

- The load is the weight of the body being lifted.
- The effort is the force applied by the gastrocnemius muscle as it contracts to pull the heel upwards.
- The lever involves the bones of the foot.
- This lever system can produce considerable force at the expense of speed and range of movement.
- This is a more efficient lever system than a third class lever system because:
  - the effort is further away from the fulcrum than the load, therefore
  - it requires a smaller effort to move an equivalent load.

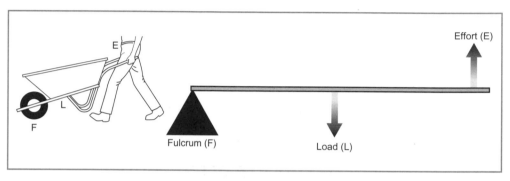

Fig. 3.25 Standing on tiptoe gives a **second class lever** system at the metatarsals/

Fig. 3.26 The load is located between the fulcrum and the effort in a second class lever system.

**KEY WORDS**

Second class lever

Third class lever

Third class lever system

- The effort is located between the fulcrum and the load.
- This is the most common lever system found in the body.
- An example is found in flexion of the elbow joint.
- The fulcrum is the elbow joint.
- The load is the weight of the lower arm and any resistance being applied.
- The effort is the force applied by the biceps brachii muscle as it contracts to flex the elbow.
- The lever is the radius.
- This lever system can move a load at speed through a large range of movement.
- This is a less efficient lever system than a second class lever system because:
  - the effort is closer to the fulcrum than the load, therefore
  - it takes more effort to move an equivalent load.

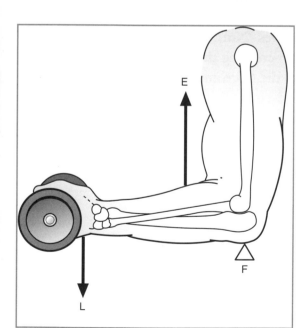

Fig. 3.27 Flexion of the elbow joint is a **third class lever** system.

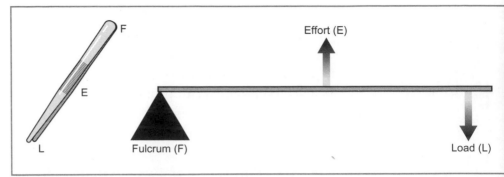

Fig. 3.28 The effort is located between the fulcrum and the load in a third class lever system

Length of lever

- Longer levers can generate greater forces which can give greater acceleration to objects that are thrown or hit. For example when serving in tennis, players are encouraged to hit the ball with the arm fully extended to gain maximum power.
- Athletes with longer limbs are at an advantage.

4 Principle of moments

Moment of force

- **Moment of force** is also known as **torque**.
- It causes a turning effect produced by the force as the lever rotates about the fulcrum.
- Moment of force = force × perpendicular distance from fulcrum.
- Moment of force = $F \times d$.
- It is measured in Newton metres (Nm).
- Generating a larger force or increasing the distance of the point of application of the force from the fulcrum will increase the moment of force.

For example, using Figure 3.29, calculate the moment of force as an athlete lowers a dumbbell in the final stages of the downward phase of a biceps curl.

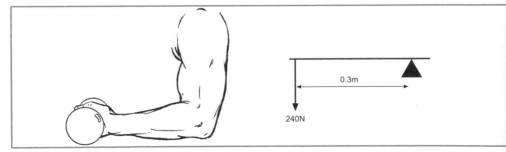

Fig. 3.29 The moment of force caused by a dumbbell in the final stages of an athlete performing the downward phase of a biceps curl.

Moment of force = force × perpendicular distance from fulcrum

= 240N × 0.3m

= 72Nm

The **principle of moments** states that, for a balanced system, the moment of force acting in a clockwise direction is equal to the moment of force acting in an anticlockwise direction.

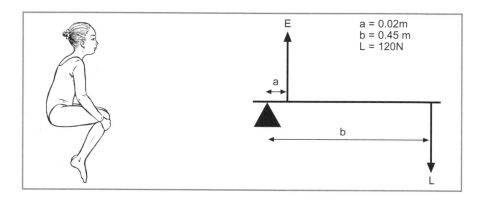

$$a = 0.02m$$
$$b = 0.45\ m$$
$$L = 120N$$

Fig. 3.30 A gymnast creating a balanced lever system about the hip joint.

For a balanced system, the principle of moments states:

Clockwise moments of force = anticlockwise moments of force

$$L \times b = E \times a$$
$$120N \times 0.45m = E \times 0.02m$$
$$E = 54/0.02$$
$$E = 2700N$$

5 Principle axes of rotation

- An **axis of rotation** is an imaginary line or point about which a body rotates.
- For example, the leg rotates about the hip when kicking a football.
- A **principle axis of rotation** is an axis directed through a human body's centre of mass.
- There are three principle axes of rotation:
  1 The **longitudinal axis of rotation** passes from head to foot.
     For example, a trampolinist completing a full twist jump.
  2 The **transverse axis of rotation** passes from left to right.
     For example, a diver performing a back somersault.
  3 The **frontal axis of rotation** passes from front to back.
     For example, a gymnast performing a side somersault (like a cartwheel).

KEY WORDS

Frontal axis of rotation

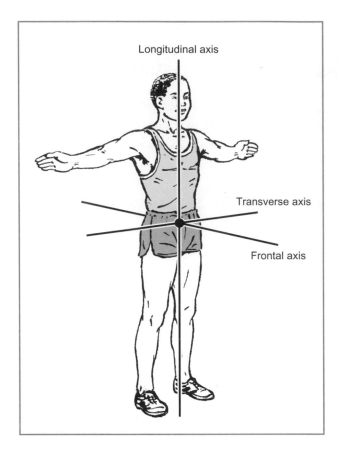

Fig. 3.31 The principle axes of rotation of a body pass through the centre of mass.

6 Measurements used in angular motion

KEY WORDS

Angular distance

Radians

Angular displacement

Angular distance

- **Angular distance** is the angle (θ) through which a body has rotated about an axis in moving from the first position to the second.
- It is a scalar quantity.
- It is measured in degrees or **radians**.

Angular displacement

- **Angular displacement** is the smallest angular change (θ) between the starting and finishing positions.
- It is a vector quantity.
- It is measured in degrees or radians.

Angular speed

- **Angular speed** is the rate of change of angular distance (how fast a body is spinning).

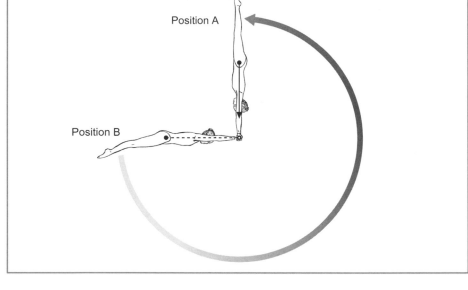

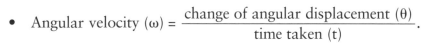

Fig. 3.32 In rotating from position A to position B, the gymnast has an angular distance of 4.7rad (270°), but an angular displacement of 1.5rad (90°).

- **Angular speed** (ω) = $\dfrac{\text{change of angular distance } (\theta)}{\text{time taken } (t)}$.

$$\omega = \frac{\theta}{t}$$

- It is measured in radians per second (rads⁻¹).
- It is a scalar quantity.

Angular velocity

- **Angular velocity** is the rate of change of angular displacement (how fast a body is spinning and in which direction).

- Angular velocity (ω) = $\dfrac{\text{change of angular displacement } (\theta)}{\text{time taken } (t)}$.

$$(\omega) = \frac{\theta}{t}$$

- It is measured in radians per second (rad/s).
- It is a vector quantity.

For example, when the legs of a trampolinist performing a seat drop rotate 1.5 radians in 0.6 seconds, then the average angular velocity can be calculated as follows:

Angular velocity (ω) = $\dfrac{\text{change of angular displacement}}{\text{time}}$.

$$= \frac{1.5}{0.6}$$
$$= 2.5 \text{ rads}$$

Angular acceleration

- **Angular acceleration** is the rate of change of angular velocity.

- Angular acceleration $(\varpi) = \dfrac{\text{change of angular velocity } (\omega)}{\text{time taken } (t)}$.

$$(\varpi) = \frac{\omega}{t}$$

- It is measured in radians per second squared (rads^{-2}).
- It is a vector quantity.

For example, when the angular velocity of a gymnast performing a somersault increases from 5 rads^{-1} to 15 rads^{-2} in a time of 0.5 seconds, we can work out the angular acceleration of the gymnast as follows:

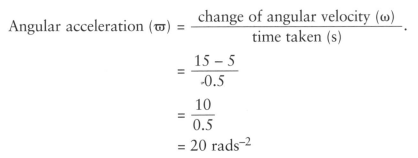

Angular acceleration $(\varpi) = \dfrac{\text{change of angular velocity } (\omega)}{\text{time taken } (s)}$.

$$= \frac{15 - 5}{-0.5}$$

$$= \frac{10}{0.5}$$

$$= 20 \text{ rads}^{-2}$$

7 Angular analogues of Newton's Laws

The difference in Newton's Laws when applied to rotating bodies lies only in the terminology used.

Angular analogue of Newton's First Law of Motion

❝ *A rotating body continues to turn about its axis of rotation with a constant angular momentum unless acted upon by an external torque.* ❞

For example, a spinning ice skater will continue to rotate until she lands, when the ice exerts an external torque on her skates to change her state of angular momentum.

This helps us to explain how an athlete, such as a spinning ice skater, is able to control their angular velocity and is discussed further on pp. 99–101. For a body to start rotating an external torque/moment of force needs to be applied.

For example, an ice skater will ensure that the reaction force applied to her from the ice will pass outside her centre of mass to create the torque to give her some angular momentum.

Angular analogue of Newton's Second Law of Motion

❝ *When a torque acts on a body, the rate of change of angular momentum experienced by the body is proportional to the size of the torque and takes place in the direction in which the torque acts.* **"**

The larger the torque/moment of force, the greater the change in angular momentum.

Angular analogue of Newton's Third Law of Motion

' *For every torque that is exerted by one body on another there is an equal and opposite torque exerted by the second body on the first.* **'**

For example, a diver will apply a downward and right-hand torque to the diving board, which in turn will generate an upward and left-hand torque on the diver allowing him to take off from the board and twist to his left.

8 Moment of inertia

- **Moment of inertia** is the resistance of a body to rotate (or its resistance to stop rotating once undergoing angular motion).
- The larger the moment of inertia (I), the harder it is to rotate (or stop rotating once undergoing angular motion).

HOT TIPS

To decide on whether a rotating body has a high or low moment of inertia, it is very important to first identify the axis of rotation.

For example, it is easier to learn a tucked somersault before a straight somersault.

Two factors determine the size of the moment of inertia:

1   The mass of the body: the larger the mass of a body, the greater its moment of inertia.

2   The distribution of the mass of the body from the axis of rotation: the further the distribution of mass from the axis of rotation, the greater the moment of inertia.

For example, a gymnast will have a higher moment of inertia about their transverse axis of rotation when performing a straight somersault than when performing a tucked somersault.

- $I = \sum mr^2$ (where r is the distance from the axis of rotation).
- It is measured in kgm^2 (kilogrammes metres/ squared).
- It is a scalar quantity.
- Once a body is rotating, it is possible to change its moment of inertia.

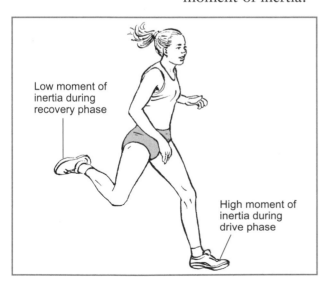

Low moment of inertia during recovery phase

High moment of inertia during drive phase

Fig. 3.33 A low moment of inertia of the leg during the recovery phase in sprinting allows the athlete to bring the leg through easily and quickly.

For example, when an ice skater is spinning about her longitudinal axis with her arms stretched out to the side, she can reduce her moment of inertia by bringing her arms back into her body.

KEY WORDS

Angular momentum

Law of conservation of angular momentum

9 Angular momentum

- **Angular momentum** is the quantity of angular motion possessed by a rotating body.
- Angular momentum is generated when a torque is applied to a body.
- Angular momentum = moment of inertia × angular velocity.
- $AM = I\omega$.
- It is measured in kilograms metres/squared per second, kgm^2/s.

Law of conservation of angular momentum

- The **Law of conservation of constant angular momentum** is a result of the analogue of Newton's First Law of Motion.
- This states that 'a rotating body continues to turn about its axis of rotation with constant angular momentum unless acted upon by an external torque'.

This means that, for rotating athletes, they can:

- increase their angular velocity by decreasing their moment of inertia – pull their bodies in to rotate faster
- decrease their angular velocity by increasing their moment of inertia – spread their bodies to rotate slower.

Application of the law of conservation of angular momentum to a diver
Consider a diver who takes off from the board to complete one and a half back somersaults as shown in Figure 3.34.

Take off:

- Transverse axis of rotation.
- Angular momentum is generated at take off by the diver applying a downward and forward torque to the diving board and the board generating an upward and backward torque on the diver (analogue of Newton's Third Law).
- The diver ensures a large moment of inertia by maintaining a straight body position.
- This generates a large angular momentum even though angular velocity is small.

During flight:

- The amount of angular momentum at take off remains the same during flight until the diver hits the water (analogue of Newton's First Law).

- The diver reduces his moment of inertia by tucking his body in.
- This increases his rate of spin (angular velocity) to enable him to complete his one and half turns before he hits the water.

Prior to landing/entry into the water:

- The diver increases his moment of inertia by straightening his body out.
- This decreases his rate of spin (angular velocity) towards the end of the dive.
- This controls his entry into the water and prevents over-rotation.

Landing/entry into the water:

- Angular momentum is eliminated during landing/entry by the water applying an opposite torque to the diver's motion so that the diver stops rotating altogether.

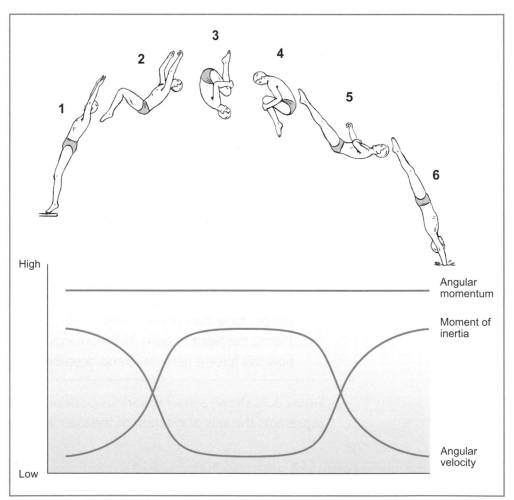

HOT TIPS

Gymnasts, trampolinists, ice skaters, slalom skiers and discus throwers are other athletes who use the law of conservation of momentum just like divers.

Fig. 3.34 A diver makes use of the conservation of angular momentum.

CHECK!

Go back to the overview diagrams on pp. 1, 68 and 90. If you are satisfied with your knowledge and understanding, tick off the sections that you have revised so far. If you are not satisfied, then revisit those sections and refer to the pages in the 'Need to know more?'

Exam practice

1 Figure 3.35 shows the relationship between the velocity and time of the descent of a ski jumper down the ramp prior to take off.

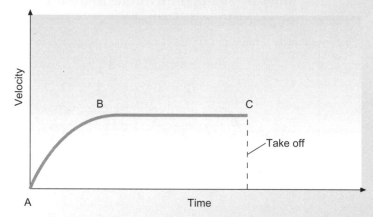

Fig. 3.35

(a) Describe the motion of the ski jumper during the descent and use Newton's First Law of Motion to explain the shape of the curve between points B and C. **(4 marks)**

(b) Identify the forces acting against the ski jumper between points B and C. Explain the reasons behind the methods used by the ski jumper to reduce these forces. **(4 marks)**

(c) During the flight phase a lift force can act on the ski jumper. Explain how this force is generated and describe its effect. **(4 marks)**

2 Figure 3.36 shows a skier in various positions. The broken line represents the axis of rotation of the skier when turning.

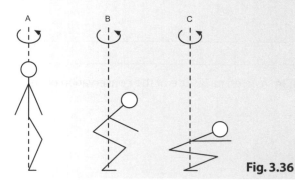

Fig. 3.36

(a) With reference to Figure 3.36 (A), identify the axis through which the skier rotates. **(1 mark)**

(b) Describe how a slalom skier uses the law of conservation of angular momentum to aid his technique at the start, during and end of a turn. **(6 marks)**

3 Figure 3.37 shows a diagram of the foot of a basketball player pivoting at a point under the ball of the foot.

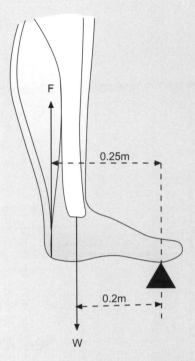

Fig. 3.37

(a) If the mass of the basketball player is 100kg, calculate his weight w and the moment of force caused by the weight. (Assume acceleration due to gravity is 10m/s^2). Show all your working. **(3 marks)**

(b) Use your knowledge of the principle of moments applied to this lever system to calculate force. Explain why the ankle is one of the most efficient lever systems in the body. **(4 marks)**

(c) Use Newton's Laws of Motion to explain how the basketball player would take off when jumping for the ball. If the (normal) reaction force applied to the basketball player is 1500N, calculate the vertical acceleration experienced at take off. **(7 marks)**

4 Explain the concept of centre of mass. Describe how a basketball player could manipulate the position of the centre of mass during take off and during flight in order to jump for the ball efficiently. **(7 marks)**

Now go to p. 175 to check your answers.

Chapter 4 **Sport psychology**

Chapter overview

1　Personality ☐

2　Attitudes and achievement motivation ☐

3　Group dynamics of sport performance ☐

4　Mental preparation for sport performance ☐

5　Competition effects on sport performance ☐

6　Consequences of sport performance ☐

Tick the box when you are satisfied with your level of knowledge and understanding for each section within this chapter.

Section 1: *Personality*

Section overview

1　Introduction ☐

2　What is personality? ☐

3　Psychodynamic theory ☐

4　Trait, social learning and interactionist theories ☐

NEED TO KNOW MORE?

For further information on personality, see pp. 219–22 in *Advanced PE for OCR: A2.*

Tick the box when you are satisfied with your level of knowledge and understanding for each topic within this section.

1 Introduction

Personality is:
- stable
- enduring
- unique to each individual.

- Personality determines the way an individual responds to the environment.
- Therefore, it is the key to optimising performance and a link between all components of this syllabus.

Personality involves:
- character
- temperament
- intellect
- physique.

NEED TO KNOW MORE?

For further information on TAS personalities, see pp. 111–12 of this book.

Here are examples of responses determined by environmental circumstances. Note how they link together

Concentration
The capacity to focus and maintain focus is dependent upon:
- personality and arousal levels
- preferred style of attention.

Control
- Optimal performance relies on focus and concentration.
- Some personalities attain peak flow experiences under conditions of high arousal.

Commitment
Certain personality characteristics enable some individuals to accept challenges. TAS characters commit to challenges and are:
- most confident
- optimally aroused when the chance of success is 50/50.

Confidence
- Level of confidence facilitates optimal performance.
- Confident personalities:
  - control emotion
  - concentrate more easily
  - commit to challenges.

KEY WORDS

Perception

Cognition

Arousal

Activation

Personality influences:

- **perception**: the interpretation an individual gives to environmental information
- **cognition**: the process of thought.

Personality associates with:

- **arousal**: a physical and mental state of preparedness
- **activation**: a condition that reflects the degree of physical readiness.

2 What is personality?

❛ *Personality is the sum total of an individual's characteristics which make him unique.* ❜
(Hollander)

Hollander (1967) presented a model comprising three concentric rings representing the structure of personality.

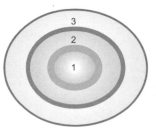

Fig. 4.01 Concentric

1 **The psychological core** – this is the 'real you'.
   - The core stores the concept of true self and is never revealed.
   - Tests cannot penetrate the core, so accurate prediction of personality cannot be made.
2 **Typical responses** – represents the usual manner in which a response to an environmental situation is made.
   - A typical response is learned and is the product of accumulated experience.
   - This may indicate an attitude; for example, an inclination toward **'learned helplessness'**. This is the belief that failure is inevitable.
3 **Role-related behaviour** – this is the surface of personality.
   - Role-related behaviour is determined by our perception of the environment at any given moment in time.
   - This may explain irrational responses; for example, an act of **aggression**. This involves the intention to harm another person.

3 Psychodynamic theory

This theory was presented by Freud (1933). He believed that three components of personality interact to produce individual patterns of behaviour which can arise in sport.

According to this theory, personality is formed because of a permanent state of psychological conflict between seeking, releasing and inhibiting behaviour.

Fig. 4.02 The coach must work hard to develop the super ego of these players. In this situation there is a strong possibility that that the ego will release the behaviour desired by the id. The response may be dysfunctional.

HOT TIPS

All psychology theories must relate to sport. Practical examples are often required in an exam answer.

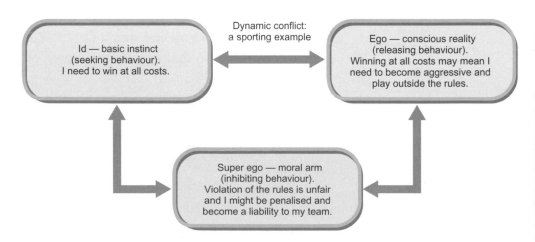

Dynamic conflict: a sporting example

Id — basic instinct (seeking behaviour). I need to win at all costs.

Ego — conscious reality (releasing behaviour). Winning at all costs may mean I need to become aggressive and play outside the rules.

Super ego — moral arm (inhibiting behaviour). Violation of the rules is unfair and I might be penalised and become a liability to my team.

Fig. 4.03 Psychodynamic theory.

4 Trait, social learning and interactionist theories

HOT TIPS

The approach to personality formation indicated by the three views shown in this table is the one most likely to appear in the examination.

HOT TIPS

Be aware of the strengths and drawbacks of each perspective.

KEY WORDS

Neurotic

Extrovert

Stable

Introvert

Trait

Trait theory

Social learning theory

Interactionist theory

Trait theory of personality	Social learning theory of personality	Interactionist theory of personality
• Personality is a product of nature. • A **trait** is a characteristic of personality, which is inherited by a child at birth. • Traits are considered to be innate forces or instincts causing an individual to act in a certain way. • Cattell identified 16 groups of traits, which he claimed were present within all people at varying degrees of intensity. • Traits are arranged in hierarchical form with the primary or strongest overriding weaker or secondary traits. • Eysenck stated that the traits most likely to be displayed should be known as the personality type. • Eysenck recognised four personality types: 1 **Neurotic** and **extroverted** 2 **Stable** and extroverted 3 Stable and **introverted** 4 Neurotic and introverted	• Personality is a product of nurture. • This theory suggests that all behaviour is learned through interaction with the environment. • Therefore, the response made by an individual cannot be predicted. • Bandura believed that learning takes place in two ways: 1 First, we tend to imitate the behaviour of others through observation. This is referred to as modelling. 2 Second, new behaviours are acquired when they are endorsed through social reinforcement.	• Personality is a product of both nature and nurture. • This approach considers both the inherited characteristics and the environmental influences in the development of personality. • This theory combines trait and social learning theories and is generally accepted to be a more realistic explanation of personality. • A psychologist named Bowers went so far as to claim, 'Interaction between the person and the situation explains twice as much as traits and situations alone.' • Each personality theory has been presented as a result of careful assessment. There are several distinctive ways to test behaviour most commonly exhibited.
Drawbacks of this theory **Trait theory** is an unreliable predictor of behaviour. Trait theory does not take into account environmental experiences.	*Drawbacks of this theory* The weakness of **social learning theory** is that it takes little account of inherited behaviours.	*Strength of this theory* **Interactionist theory** takes into account innate characteristics and environmental influences
Equation B = F(P) Behaviour = Function of Personality	Equation B = F(E) Behaviour = Function of Environment	Equation B = F(PE) Behaviour = Function of Personality × Environment

Eynsenck's personality types

Eysenck recognised four personality types:

1   Neurotic and extroverted
2   Stable and extroverted

3   Stable and introverted

4   Neurotic and introverted.

Eynsenck's personality types are presented on a two-dimensional model:

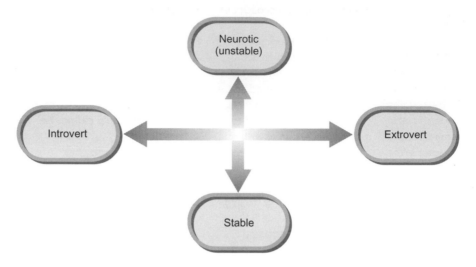

Fig. 4.04 Personality types.

HOT TIPS

Be aware of the problems associated with personality profiling.

Arising from trait perspective is the 'narrow band' approach of personality presented by Girdano (1990). Narrow band identifies two personality types which are genetically inherited.

Type A characteristics	Type B characteristics
• Highly competitive	• Non-competitive
• Strong desire to succeed	• Unambitious
• Works fast	• Works more slowly
• Likes to control	• Does not enjoy control
• Prone to suffer stress	• Less prone to stress

 CHECK !

Go back to the overview diagrams on p. 104. If you are satisfied with your knowledge and understanding, tick off the sections that you have revised so far. If you are not satisfied, then revisit those sections and refer to the pages in the 'Need to know more?'

Section 2: *Attitudes*

Section overview

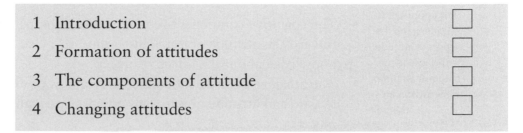

1 Introduction ☐
2 Formation of attitudes ☐
3 The components of attitude ☐
4 Changing attitudes ☐

 **NEED TO KNOW MORE?**

For further information on attitudes, see pp. 227–35 in *Advanced PE for OCR: A2*.

Tick the box when you are satisfied with your level of knowledge and understanding for each topic within this section.

1 Introduction

 KEY WORDS

Attitude

Attitude object

A mode of behaviour that is thought to be a typical response from an individual is termed an **attitude**. An attitude:

- is invariably associated with personality and is frequently used to explain a mannerism or a response in a given situation
- is an enduring emotional and behavioural response
- is unstable
- can be changed and controlled.

The **attitude object** is the subject toward which the attitude is directed.

2 Formation of attitudes

- Attitudes are formed through experiences.
- A pleasant experience in PE is likely to promote a positive attitude towards sport.
- Parents have an initial impact in attitude formation.
- The teacher or coach could be influential.
- In teenage years the **peer group**, an immediate group of friends, has the most powerful influence.
- The process of interaction between individuals and groups of people is called **socialisation**.

 KEY WORDS

Peer group

Socialisation

Prejudice

Negative prejudice

Positive prejudice

Problems associated with established attitudes:

- Attitudes can bring about false perceptions.
- **Prejudice** is a prejudgement arising from an evaluation based on inadequate information and can be **negative prejudice** or **positive predudice**.

3 The components of attitude

The triadic model of attitudes

An attitude comprises three components:

- The cognitive component represents the thinking part of an opinion towards an attitude object. This component also reflects beliefs and knowledge about the affective object.
- The affective component consists of feelings or an emotional response towards an attitude object. This component evaluates an attitude object.
- The behavioural component concerns how a person intends to behave towards an attitude object.

4 Changing attitudes

Cognitive dissonance theory

- This theory predicts that if a person holds two opposing ideas, emotion conflict or **dissonance** arises.
- To reduce this feeling of dissonance, the impact of one of the conflicting ideas could be lessened.
- Altering any one of the three components of attitude can bring about a change.

Persuasive communication theory

There are four elements to persuasive communication theory.

1 The persuader	2 The message	3 The recipients	4 The situation
This person needs to be perceived as significant and to have high status	The message needs to be presented in a way that makes the recipient want to change an attitude	The attitude is more easily changed if the recipient really wishes to be changed	Attitudes are easier to change if there are other persuaders present

- As attitudes become more specific, they are more likely to predict behaviour.
- The most effective predictor of behaviour is behavioural intention.

Achievement motivation

- Achievement motivation is the extent to which an individual is motivated to attain success.

- Achievement motivation links personality with competitiveness.
- Competitive motivation is generated through a combination of personality and the situational factors (Atkinson and McClelland's interactionist view of achievement motivation).

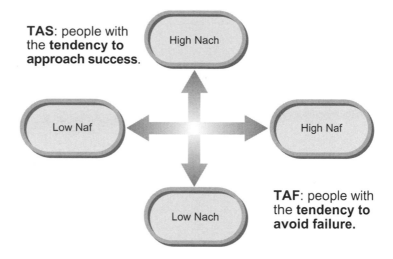

TAS: people with the **tendency to approach success**.

TAF: people with the **tendency to avoid failure**.

Fig. 4.05 Atkinson and McClelland's interactionist view of achievement motivation.

TAS personality characteristics	TAF personality characteristics
High need to achieve	Low need to achieve
Low need to avoid failure	High need to avoid failure
Highly competitive	Uncompetitive
Accept challenge	Decline challenge
Unconcerned about failure	Worried about failure
Failure attributed to external factors	Failure attributed to internal factors
Confidence maintained in failure	Confidence lost in failure
Success attributed to internal factors	Success attributed to external factors
Confidence endorsed through success	Success does not boost confidence
High expectation of success	High expectation of failure
Mastery orientation (strong motive to succeed	Learned helplessness

The situational factors that determine competitiveness involve:

- the **probability of success** when a challenge is undertaken
- the resulting **incentive value** if success is attained.

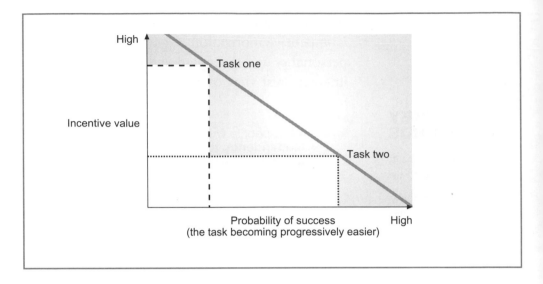

Fig. 4.06 The relationship between probability of success and incentive value give the situational factors which determine competitiveness.

TAS personalities tend to choose tasks with a lower probability of success.

- This indicates the acceptance of a difficult task/challenge.
- Confirms 'approach behaviour'.
- TAS people experience highest motivation when there is a 50 per cent chance of success and therefore adopt approach behaviours.

See also somatic and cognitive responses to anxiety and peak flow state on pp. 127–8.

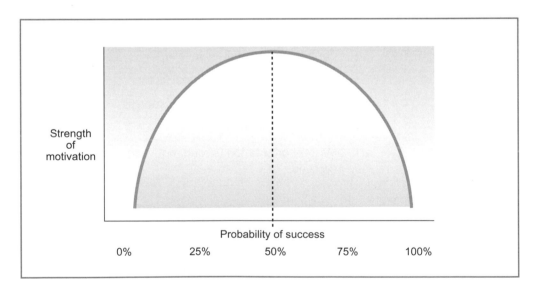

Fig. 4.07 Interactionist model of achievement.

NEED TO KNOW MORE?

For further information on achievement motivation, see pp. 231–34 in *Advanced PE for OCR: A2.*

TAF personalities tend to choose tasks with a higher probability of success.

- This indicates an inclination to take on an easy task.
- Confirms 'avoidance behaviour'.
- TAF people experience greatest anxiety when there is a 50 per cent probability of failure and therefore adopt avoidance behaviours.

See also somatic and cognitive responses to anxiety and peak flow state on pp. 127–8.

 CHECK !

Go back to the overview diagrams on pp. 104 and 109. If you are satisfied with your knowledge and understanding, tick off the sections that you have revised so far. If you are not satisfied, then revisit those sections and refer to the pages in the 'Need to know more?'

HOT TIPS

There is no link between extraversion/introversion and TAS Personality characteristics. Do not confuse type A + B personalities with TAS/TAF.

NEED TO KNOW MORE?

For further information on group dynamics of sport performance, see pp. 236–46 in *Advanced PE for OCR: A2.*

Section 3: *Group dynamics of sport performance*

Section overview

1 Introduction	☐
2 Steiner's model	☐
3 Leadership	☐

Tick the box when you are satisfied with your level of knowledge and understanding for each topic within this section.

1 Introduction

KEY WORDS

Group dynamics

All successful teams tend to work together to achieve a goal. Therefore, the coach must understand the social processes operating within a group. This interaction between team members is called **group dynamics**.

Sports teams or groups which interact well have three common characteristics:

- a collective identity
- a sense of shared purpose
- a clear structure for communication.

KEY WORDS

Group cohesion

Group cohesion describes the degree of successful bonding or the strength of collective group co-operation.

There are two types of cohesion.

1   Task cohesion:

- relates to the way in which team members work with each other to complete a task successfully; for example, to win the match
- is necessary for **interactive sports**; for example, netball.

2   Social cohesion:

- involves personal relationships within the group, for example a touring team often develops strong social bonds
- is important for **co-active sports** when the individual performs alone; for example, track and field.

Within a large group such as a hockey squad, **sub-groups** may develop.

Sub-groups:

- damage the development of a cohesive team
- comprise cliques, reciprocal pairs, isolates and rejectees.

The coach should be aware of sub-groups and adopt measures to unite the whole group.

2 Steiner's model

Steiner presented a model to explain the relationship between an interactive group and its performance in sport.

Actual Productivity = Potential Productivity – losses due to Faulty Processes

- Actual productivity is the team performance at a given time during the game or event and refers the extent of successful interaction.
- Potential productivity is the maximum capability of the group when cohesiveness is strongest.
- Faulty processes relate to the factors that can go wrong in team performance, which will impede or even prevent group cohesion and detract from the collective potential of the team.

There are two faulty processes that bring about losses in potential productivity.

1   Co-ordination losses (the Ringlemann effect).
- These losses occur because the operational effectiveness of the group as a unit cannot be sustained for the duration of a match.
- The synchronisation of teamwork breaks down.

NEED TO KNOW MORE?

For further information on sports teams or groups and their performance, see pp. 236–40 in *Advanced PE for OCR: A2.*

- Ringlemann stated that problems in team co-ordination are more likely to occur as the team numbers increase.
- Therefore, a basketball team is more likely to operate together successfully than a Rugby Union team.

2 Motivational losses ('social loafing').

- Relate to an individual who suffers a reduction of motivation during performance.
- This loss causes the player to withdraw effort and 'coast' through a period or whole game.
- Relaxation of effort is called 'social loafing' and this would detract from the cohesiveness of the team.

KEY WORDS

Group locomotion

Group cohesion is the force that binds a group together, helping to prevent faulty processes.

Group **locomotion** is the process that explains the reason why the group has formed and symbolises the activity of the team. For locomotion to be efficient there must be a leader to ensure the co-ordination of team members.

3 Leadership

The importance of effective leadership

Leadership may be considered as the process of guiding individuals and groups toward set goals.

Characteristics of an effective leader

HOT TIPS

The characteristics of effective leadership is a popular examination question and is often overlooked. It is wrongly assumed that good players automatically make good leaders.

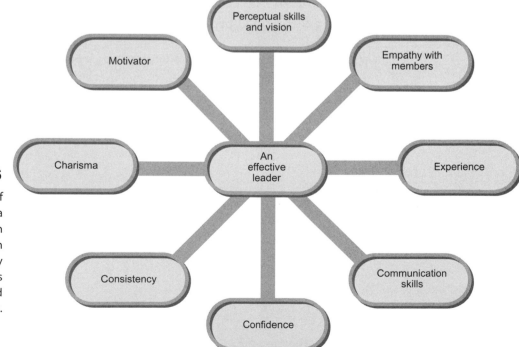

Selection of a leader

A leader can be selected in one of two ways.

- An emergent leader already belongs to the group.
- A prescribed leader is selected from outside of the group.

Styles of leadership

Fiedler's contingency model

Fiedler identified two types of leadership in his contingency model:

1 Task-orientated or autocratic leader.
   - Tends to make all of the decisions.
   - Tasks are completed as quickly as possible.
   - This style is authoritarian and takes no account of group preferences.
   - The autocratic leader will not delegate.
   - This style is effective when quick decisions are needed for large groups; for example, interactive games.
   - A task-orientated approach would be required in potentially dangerous situations.
2 Social- or person-orientated leader, also known as the democratic leader.
   - Shares the decisions with the group and is often ready to delegate responsibility.
   - This type of leader believes in consultation.
   - Develops inter-personal relationships within the team.
   - Effective in a co-active game when time constraints are not as exacting and personal support may be required.

Fiedler stated that the style of leadership depends on the 'favourableness' of the situation.

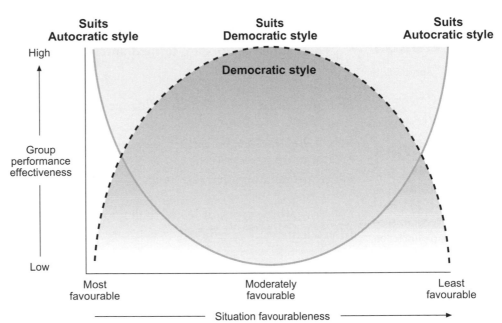

Fig. 4.08 Fiedler's leadership style and favourability of the situation.

Autocratic task-orientated leaders are more effective in both the most favourable and the least favourable situations.

Democratic person-orientated leaders are more effective in moderately favourable situations.

The multidimensional model of sports leadership

Chellanduria believed that the effectiveness of leadership could be judged upon the degree of success accomplished during a task and the extent to which the group experienced satisfaction while being led to the goal.

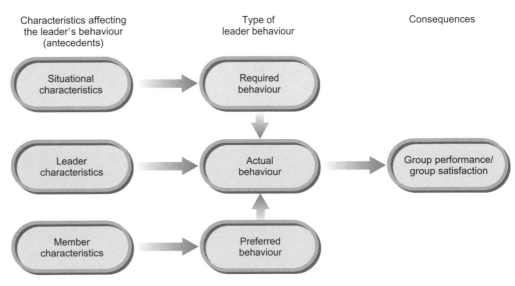

Fig. 4.09 The multidimensional model of sports leadership.

KEY WORDS

Antecedents

- Three factors interact to determine the behaviour adopted by the leader.
- These initial factors are termed **antecedents,** which are preceding circumstances.

The three antecedents which influence the leader's behaviour are:

HOT TIPS

The key to understanding the multidimensional model of sports leadership is that optimal performance and group satisfaction occurs if the leader behaviour is appropriate for the situation and suits the preference of the group.

- situational characteristics
- leader characteristics
- group member characteristics.

There are three types of leader behaviour which would be guided by the antecedents:

- required behaviour
- actual behaviour
- preferred behaviour.

KEY WORDS

Congruent

The important element of the theory is that if all three of the leader's behaviours are **congruent** (for example, antecedents, types and consequences coincide exactly), then member satisfaction and high group performance will result.

NEED TO KNOW MORE?

For further information on leadership, see pp. 240–5 in *Advanced PE for OCR: A2.*

✔ CHECK !

Go back to the overview diagrams on pp. 104 and 113. If you are satisfied with your knowledge and understanding, tick off the sections that you have revised so far. If you are not satisfied, then revisit those sections and refer to the pages in the 'Need to know more?'

Section 4: *Mental preparation for sport performance*

Section overview

NEED TO KNOW MORE?

For further information on mental preparation for sport performance, see pp. 247–60 in *Advanced PE for OCR: A2*.

Tick the box when you are satisfied with your level of knowledge and understanding for each topic within this section.

1 Introduction

Mental preparation for performance is a primary focus of sport psychology. This section presents the terms confidence, concentration and control, and attempts to demonstrate how these terms integrate to optimise performance and increase commitment.

HOT TIPS

Commitment links with achievement motivation and with TAS and TAF personality characteristics (See pp. 111–13 of this book).

- A committed performer in sport will become involved in challenges and persevere in adversity.
- Without commitment potential the performer will remain unfulfilled.
- Commitment is readily displayed after a run of success.
- Success develops confidence and with it brings the expectation of higher attainment.
- Failure would reduce confidence and cause an increase in anxiety.
- The relationship between increasing anxiety and sport performance operates on a downward spiral, resulting in learned helplessness, avoidance behaviours and a withdrawal of commitment.

Measures can be put into place to increase the level of commitment and to address the issues of confidence, concentration and control of emotion in all circumstances. One such measure is goal setting.

2 Goal setting

Types of goal

1 Outcome goals (also known as ego or ability goals) are externally controlled and concern winning or losing.

HOT TIPS

Be aware of the advantages of process goals

2 Process or performance goals (also known as task or mastery goals) are measurable results that relate directly to the performer. These goals are internally controlled.

- Process goals tend to be more flexible and relate to the effort and ability of the performer.
- It is safer to set process goals because the performer has some control over the attainment.
- To reach a performance target against oneself is a more accurate reflection of progress and commitment.

HOT TIPS

Learn SMARTER targets. This is an important guide to successful target setting.

  S **Specific** to the event or skill.

  M **Measurable** targets ensure that progress can be compared with a standard.

  A **Accepted** by the coach and the performer.

  R **Realistic** goals should be set that are challenging but within reach.

  T **Time** limitations must be in place.

  E **Exciting** goals will inspire and reward the performer.

  R **Recording** progress provides feedback and motivation: 'Ink it, don't think it'.

3 Self-confidence

> ❛ *The most consistent difference between elite and less successful athletes is that elite athletes possess greater self-confidence.* ❜
> (Gould *et al*)

KEY WORDS

Self-efficacy

Self-confidence

Attribution

As people become competent in particular skills and situations, they develop a feeling of **self-efficacy**.

- Self-efficacy relates to specific situations; for example, an otherwise confident football player may lack confidence when taking a penalty.
- Self-efficacy is a micro approach to understanding **self-confidence**.
- Self-confidence is global and applies to all situations because it is a stable personality characteristic.
- People with high self-efficacy tend to seek challenges.
- They attribute success to internal factors that relate directly to themselves, such as ability and effort.
- **Attribution** theory relates to the reasons given for success or failure.
- Internal attributions would elevate confidence and increase the expectation of success in the next challenge.

HOT TIPS

Link self-efficacy with achievement motivation, attribution and attribution retraining.

- The level of efficacy determines efficacy expectations, which directly influence the choice and commitment an individual makes regarding sporting activities.
- Efficacy expectations can be changed by an input of four major types of information, which are the sub-processes in self-efficacy theory.
- By applying each of the four sub-processes, self-efficacy can be raised.

4 Self-efficacy theory

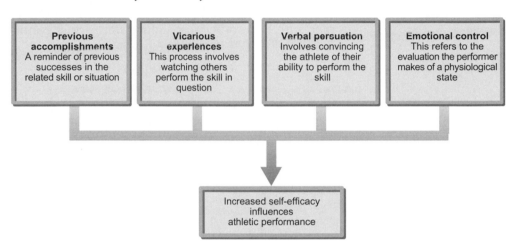

Fig. 4.10 Self-efficacy theory.

5 Sport-specific model of sport confidence

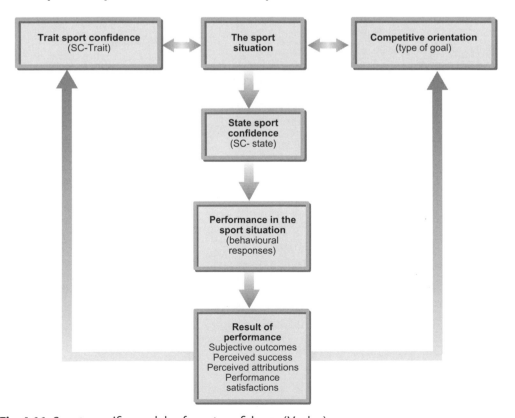

Fig. 4.11 Sport-specific models of sport confidence (Vealey).

Vealey's model relates to global sports confidence and is therefore a macro approach to the study of confidence.

KEY WORDS

Trait sport confidence

State sport confidence

- **Trait sport confidence** is the amount of confidence a person has in their overall sports ability. This tends to be stable.
- The sports situation involves the skill or situation that requires attention; for example, the race.
- Competition orientation is the type of goal that has been set.

Trait sport confidence, the sports situation and competition orientation interact with each other to produce state sport confidence.

Three facts about state sport confidence:

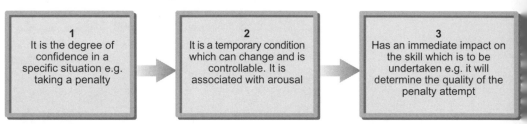

Three effects of a successful outcome:

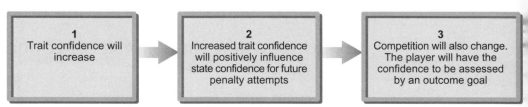

Nine ways to increase state sport confidence:

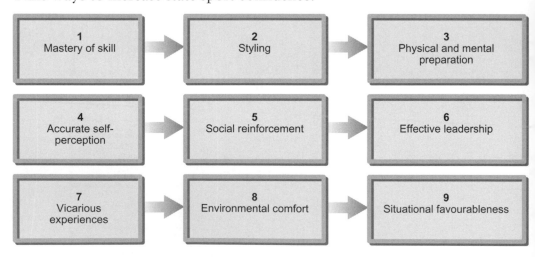

NEED TO KNOW MORE?

For further information on self-confidence, self-efficacy and the sport-specific model of sport confidence, see pp. 249–52 in *Advanced PE for OCR: A2.*

6 Concentration

- Concentration involves focusing attention onto the relevant environmental cues and maintaining attentional focus until the skill has been completed.
- Concentration can be drawn by external factors such as stimulus intensity.
- Internal processes such as cognition and the emotional condition of arousal also influence the capacity to concentrate.

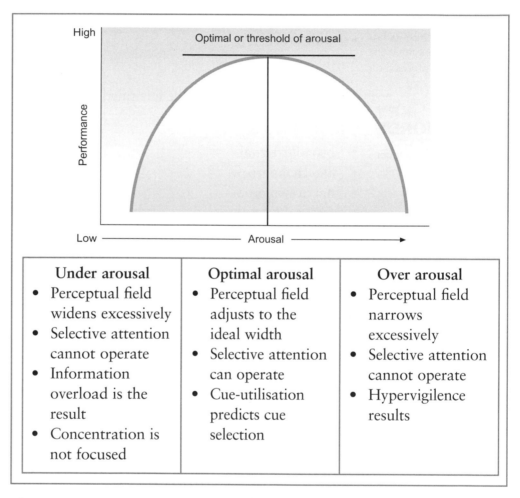

Under arousal	Optimal arousal	Over arousal
• Perceptual field widens excessively • Selective attention cannot operate • Information overload is the result • Concentration is not focused	• Perceptual field adjusts to the ideal width • Selective attention can operate • Cue-utilisation predicts cue selection	• Perceptual field narrows excessively • Selective attention cannot operate • Hypervigilence results

Fig. 4.12 As arousal increases so does the quality of performance up to a critical or optimal point. After this threshold, if arousal continues to increase, performance will deteriorate.

KEY WORDS

Activation

Increased arousal brings about a condition of **activation**.

Activation is a condition that reflects the degree of physical readiness.

Attentional styles

Although adjustment of the perceptual field explains how attentional focus is maximised, it does not make clear what happens when the **width of attention** needs to change in response to varying situations in sport. The width of attention relates to the number of environmental cues that require the performer's attention.

HOT TIPS

A synoptic question could link arousal, concentration and cue-utilisation with the models of information processing.

Nideffer identified two dimensions on to which attentional styles could be placed:

- width (broad/narrow)
- direction (internal/external).

KEY WORDS

Width of attention

Four attentional styles can be identified on Nideffer's two-dimensional model:

- broad/external
- external/narrow
- narrow/internal
- internal/broad.

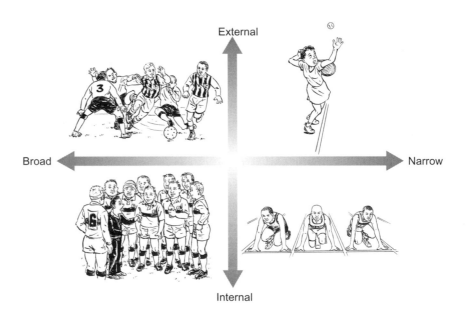

Fig. 4.13 Two-dimensional model of attention styles.

- The broad and narrow dimension (width) represents an information continuum and refers to the number of environmental cues that require attention.
- The broad extreme demands the performer to attend to many sensory cues whereas the narrow extreme requires focus onto one cue.

- On the direction dimension, external attention relates to focus as being outward and directed onto an external object.
- Internal attention refers to an inward focus onto thoughts or feelings.
- In activities in which the environment changes (for example, in an interactive game which includes open and closed skills), it may be necessary to use all four styles when appropriate.
- All performers have a preferred or strongest attentional style.
- The expert performer needs to be competent in each of the four styles.

7 Emotional control

Nothing is attained in sport without a degree of motivation.

The terms of arousal, activation and anxiety relate to motivation but need to be separately defined.

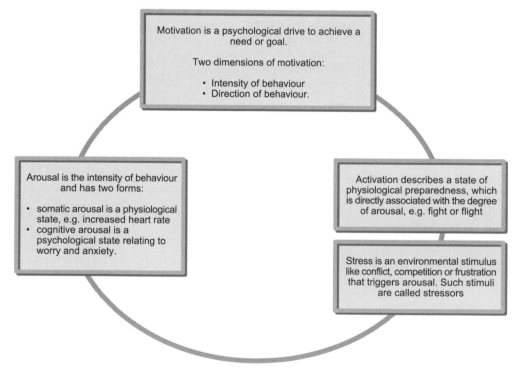

Fig. 4.14 Arousal controls the capacity to concentrate and process information.

Four factors determine the optimal point of arousal:

- personality
- task type
- stage of learning
- experience

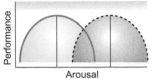

Fig. 4.13 The optimal point or threshold of arousal is different for each individual.

Introvert personality • For the introvert, optimal arousal is low on the scale. • Introverts perform best when arousal is low. • Sensitised RAS.	**Personality**	**Extrovert personality** • For the extrovert, optimal arousal is high on the scale. • Extroverts perform best when arousal is high. • Desensitised RAS.
Complex tasks • Complex tasks are performed best in conditions of low arousal. • Complex tasks are perceptual and often fine. • There is a narrow margin for error, e.g. spin bowling.	**Task type**	**Simple tasks** • Simple tasks are performed best in conditions of high arousal. • Simple tasks are ballistic. • There is a large margin for error, e.g. shot put.
Associative stage • At this stage, the learner performs best under conditions of low arousal.	**Stage of learning**	**Autonomous stage** • At this stage, the performer has become an expert. • High arousal will facilitate performance.
Novice performer • The novice performs best in conditions of low arousal.	**Experience**	**Expert performer** • The expert perfoms best in conditions of high arousal.

Fig. 4.15 The optimal point or threshold of arousal is different for each individual.

8 Individual zone of optimal functioning (IZOF)

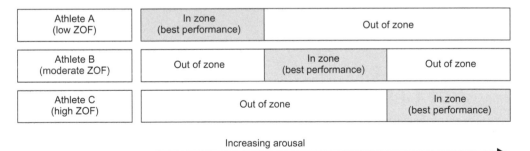

Fig. 4.16 Individual zone of optimal functioning (Hanin).

- An individual zone of optimal arousal exists in which best performance occurs.
- Outside of this zone, poor performance occurs.
- The optimal level of arousal is not a single point but a 'band width'.

The characteristics of being in the zone include:

- the performance appears effortless and automatic, with the athlete feeling in full control
- the attention and concentration of the performer is focused
- the execution of the skill brings enjoyment and satisfaction.

Entry into ZOF is also dependent on the situation matching the athlete's strongest attentional style.

9 Anxiety

Spielberger identified two sources of anxiety:

- trait anxiety – a genetically inherited and relatively stable predisposition
- state anxiety – a learned response that fluctuates in a given situation and is associated with arousal.

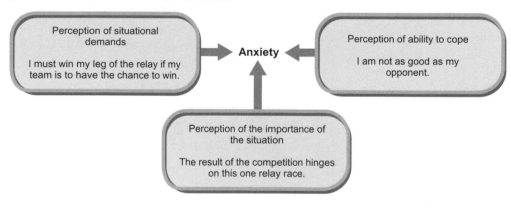

Fig. 4.17 Anxiety occurs when the performer's perception becomes imbalanced.

KEY WORDS

Somatic response

Cognitive response

Peak flow

- A **somatic response** will follow the curve of performance as predicted on the inverted U hypothesis and refers to physiological changes.
- A **cognitive response** reflects increasing worry about performance. Negative thought results.

If the athlete experiences worry, he or she will not attain a '**peak flow**' state. Peak flow occurs when all psychological and physiological variables align to give the best potential performance.

Anxiety management to improve performance

Cognitive methods include:	Somatic methods include:
• Imagery	• Progressive muscular relaxation
• Thought stopping	• Biofeedback
• Positive talk	
• Rational thinking	

Peak flow experience in sport

This condition links together the whole section relating to mental preparation for sport.

Factors that contribute to the peak flow experience:

NEED TO KNOW MORE?

For further information on emotional control, IZOF and anxiety, see pp. 255–9 in *Advanced PE for OCR: A2*.

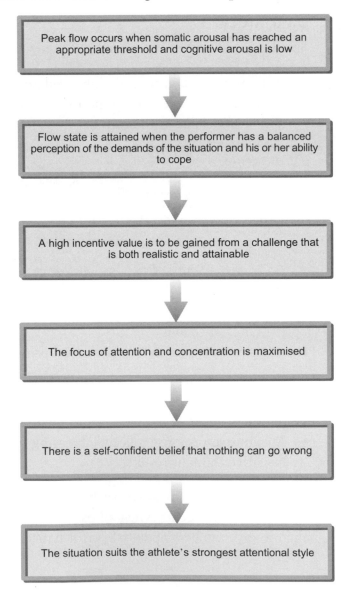

Peak flow occurs when somatic arousal has reached an appropriate threshold and cognitive arousal is low

Flow state is attained when the performer has a balanced perception of the demands of the situation and his or her ability to cope

A high incentive value is to be gained from a challenge that is both realistic and attainable

The focus of attention and concentration is maximised

There is a self-confident belief that nothing can go wrong

The situation suits the athlete's strongest attentional style

✔ **CHECK!**

Go back to the overview diagrams on pp. 104 and 119. If you are satisfied with your knowledge and understanding, tick off the sections that you have revised so far. If you are not satisfied, then revisit those sections and refer to the pages in the 'Need to know more?'

Section 5: *Competition effects on sport performance*

NEED TO KNOW MORE?

For further information on competition effects on sport performance, see pp. 260–7 in *Advanced PE for OCR: A2*.

HOT TIPS

Give clear and unquestionable examples of hostile aggression, for example a deliberate over the ball challenge in football.

HOT TIPS

Instrumental aggression is also known as channelled aggression.

Section overview

1 Aggression	☐
2 Theories of aggression	☐
3 Methods to eliminate aggressive tendencies	☐
4 Social facilitation and audience effects	☐

Tick the box when you are satisfied with your level of knowledge and understanding for each topic within this section.

1 Aggression

Three types of behaviour need to be defined before aggression can be understood

1 Hostile aggression	2 Instrumental aggression	3 Assertive behaviour
• The motive is to harm an opponent • The chief reinforcement of the aggressor is to inflict injury • Aggressive actions are outside the rules of any game • Hostile aggression is dysfunctional in the context of sport • Anger is involved	• Describes an action that is within the rules • There is intention to harm • The chief reinforcer is to complete the skill • Anger is not in evidence	• Does not attempt to harm • The chief reinforcer is to complete the skill successfully • Is strictly within the rules and spirit of the game • Involves robust play • Assertion is functional play

Antecedents of aggression in sport

An antecedent is a prior circumstance that could account for behaviour. These include:

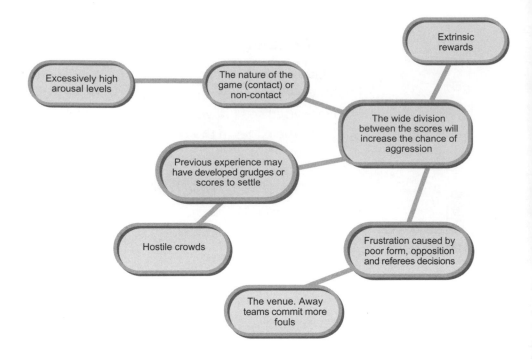

HOT TIPS

It is essential that the theories that explain the formation of aggressive behaviour can be identified and explained.

2 Theories of aggression

Trait perspective of aggression	Social learning perspective of aggression	Interactionist perspective of aggression
Instinct theory	Social learning theory	Frustration aggression hypothesis
		Aggression cue hypothesis

3 Methods to eliminate aggressive tendencies

1	Positively reinforce non-aggressive behaviour
2	Negatively reinforce aggressive behaviour
3	Punish aggressive play
4	Withdraw the aggressive player from the situation
5	Change the athlete's perception
6	Set process rather than outcome goals
7	Emphasise non-aggressive role models
8	Attribute successful performance to skilfulness and not to intimidation
9	Implement stress management techniques
10	Lower arousal levels

NEED TO KNOW MORE?

For further information on agression, see pp. 260–3 in *Advanced PE for OCR: A2.*

4 Social facilitation and audience effects

Most sports or physical activities take place in the company of other people. The presence of others influences the performance of the individual.

- The immediate effect of the presence of an audience is to increase the arousal level.
- Social facilitation occurs when the presence of an audience enhances performance.
- Social inhibition occurs when the presence of an audience impedes performance.

HOT TIPS

For exam purposes, it is essential to identify and explain five theories of social facilitation.

KEY WORDS

Dominant response

Theories of social facilitation

Identification of theory	Explanation
Drive theory	• Increases in arousal are proportional to increases in the quality of performance • The **dominant response** is the behaviour most likely to occur when arousal increases due to the presence of an audience • It is natural to experience high arousal when spectators are present
Evaluation apprehension	• The performer experiences increased levels of arousal only when the audience is perceived to be judging performance • High arousal levels due to the presence of evaluative others is a learned response
Homefield advantage	• Away teams are disadvantaged when faced by the home crowd
Distraction/conflict theory	• The added distraction of an audience is yet more competition for limited attentional space of the performer
Proximity effect	• The arousal level of the performer will increase if the location of the crowd is close to the event

HOT TIPS

A player in a sports representative trial would be assessed on outcome goals. This may evoke evaluation apprehension.

Strategies to combat social inhibition

- Practise selective attention to direct attention onto the task and cut out the awareness of others.
- Make use of cognitive visualisation techniques such as imagery and mental rehearsal to shut out the audience.
- Ensure that essential skills are over-learned and grooved as dominant responses are most likely to emerge when over-aroused.
- Introduce evaluative others into practice.

NEED TO KNOW MORE?

For further information on social faciliatation and audience effects, see pp. 264–6 in *Advanced PE for OCR: A2*.

- Simulated crowd noises, which reinforce performance positively, have proved effective in training.
- Raise the athlete's awareness of the zone of optimal functioning (ZOF).
- Incorporate stress management into training.
- Appropriate use of attribution will raise confidence when the athlete is faced with an audience.

 CHECK!

Go back to the overview diagrams on pp. 104 and 129. If you are satisfied with your knowledge and understanding, tick off the sections that you have revised so far. If you are not satisfied, then revisit those sections and refer to the pages in the 'Need to know more?'

Section 6: *Consequences of sport performance*

Section overview

NEED TO KNOW MORE?

For further information on the consequences of sport performance, see pp. 267–9 in *Advanced PE for OCR: A2*.

1 Attribution theory ☐

2 Weiner's attribution model ☐

3 Attribution retraining ☐

Tick the box when you are satisfied with your level of knowledge and understanding for each topic within this section.

1 Attribution theory

The topic of attribution looks at the common reasons given by coaches and players to account for their successes and failures in sport. Attribution is very powerful as it influences confidence and commitment.

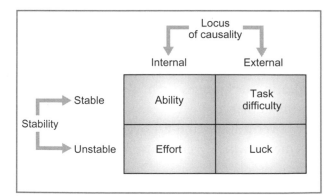

Fig. 4.18 Weiner's attribution model.

2 Weiner's attribution model

- Knowledge of attribution can endorse the confidence and expectations of successful performers.
- Attribution can prevent learned helplessness and change personality characteristics of TAF to TAS.
- The coach should look to attribute defeat to external attributions in order to sustain confidence and to establish a winning expectation.

- Such factors take away the responsibility of the loss from the players.
- This would maintain self-esteem, sustain motivation and restore pride and confidence.
- Internal attributions should reinforce victory, as this would elevate confidence and endorse a 'win' expectation.

TAF personalities

- People who are low achievers tend to attribute a lack of success to internal factors. This would take away confidence and reduce expectation of future success.
- Learned helplessness would develop and avoidance behaviour would result.
- The same people tend to attribute success to external factors.
- Confidence and expectation of attainment in the future would be reduced.

TAS personalities

- High achievers would attribute their success to internal factors and therefore seek more difficult challenges.
- Failures are put down to external variables.
- The high achiever is more persistent in the face of failure and develops **mastery orientation** (the strong motive to succeed found in the high achiever).

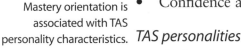

HOT TIPS

Mastery orientation is associated with TAS personality characteristics.

KEY WORDS

Mastery orientation

3 Attribution retraining

KEY WORDS

Attribution retraining

- Failure is attributed to internal, unstable and controllable factors, that is, the factors in the bottom left-hand corner of the attribution model (see Figure 4.18).
- Control over failure is given to the athlete; for example, effort attributions – with more effort the performer can succeed.

Several other attributions belong to the internal, unstable 'box of control'.

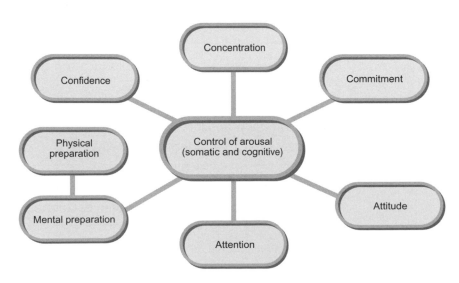

CHECK !

Go back to the overview diagrams on pp. 1, 104 and 132. If you are satisfied with your knowledge and understanding, tick off the sections that you have revised so far. If you are not satisfied, then revisit those sections and refer to the pages in the 'Need to know more?'

Exam practice

1   The use of personality as a predictor of behaviour in sport is not totally accepted by some psychologists. Identify the characteristics associated with Type A and Type B personalities.   **(4 marks)**

2   Identify the characteristics of *either* an extroverted or an introverted personality. By referring only to your choice, explain why the coach would take personality type into account during training.   **(4 marks)**

3   The attitudes and prejudices we bring in physical education or sport can have a significant impact on performance. Explain the triadic model of attitudes and describe how knowledge of this model can help to change an attitude.   **(4 marks)**

4   Use practical examples to explain the term 'learned helplessness'.   **(4 marks)**

5   Using Steiner's model, explain why a sports team might not always reach its potential. (Adapted question)   **(3 marks)**

6   Fiedler's contingency model of leadership focuses on leadership style and situation favourableness. Name and explain the two leadership styles in Fiedler's model.   **(2 marks)**

7   Use an example from physical education or sport to describe a highly favourable situation.   **(4 marks)**

8   By using a practical example to support your answer, explain the four attentional styles identified by Nideffer.   **(4 marks)**

9   Select three sources of sports confidence as identified by Vealey and use a practical example to explain each one.   **(3 marks)**

10 What strategies might a coach use to promote mastery orientation?

(4 marks)

11 Explain the factors that could affect performance when playing in front of a large crowd at an important local match. **(4 marks)**

Now go to page 178 to check your answers.

Unit 5: Exercise physiology and the integration of knowledge of principles and concepts across different areas of Physical Education

Unit Overview

Chapter 5: Exercise and sport physiology ☐

Tick the box when you are satisfied with your level of knowledge and understanding for this chapter. .

Chapter 5: **Exercise and sport physiology**

Chapter overview

1 Energy ☐

2 The recovery process ☐

3 Principles of training ☐

4 Components of fitness and improving performance ☐

5 Ergogenic aids ☐

Tick the box when you are satisfied with your level of knowledge and understanding for each section within this chapter.

Section 1: Energy

Section overview

1 Energy concepts and the role of ATP ☐

2 The phosphocreatine (ATP–PC) system ☐

3 The lactic acid system ☐

4 The aerobic system ☐

5 The energy continuum ☐

6 Thresholds ☐

NEED TO KNOW MORE?

For further information on energy, see pp. 270–9 in *Advanced PE for OCR: A2.*

Tick the box when you are satisfied with your level of knowledge and understanding for each topic within this section.

KEY WORDS

Energy

Force

Power

1 Energy concepts and the role of ATP

You need to be able to define the following **energy** concepts:

- **Energy** is the ability to perform work. Measured in joules (J).
- Work is **force** × distance. Measured in either joules (J) or Newtons (N).
- **Power** is work/time. Measured in watts (W).

Three types of energy are important:

- Kinetic energy – seen in movement; for example, running.
- Chemical energy – stored in a molecule or compound; for example, carbohydrates.
- Potential energy – due to position; for example, the high energy bond between the last two phosphate groups in a molecule of ATP.

KEY WORDS

ATP

ATPase

Adenosine triphosphate (**ATP**) is the only readily available, useable source of energy in the muscle cell. All other forms must be converted into ATP to provide energy for muscle contraction.

HOT TIPS

Know the names of some enzymes. Anything ending in '-ase' is usually an enzyme. They are easy exam marks!

ATP is only stored in small amounts and so it needs to be re-synthesised if movement is to continue. ATP is broken down by the enzyme **ATPase** to form adenosine diphosphate (ADP) and a phosphate group. This is an exothermic reaction. The body has three systems for providing ATP re-synthesis: the phosphocreatine system, the lactic acid system and the aerobic system.

2 The phosphocreatine (ATP-PC) system

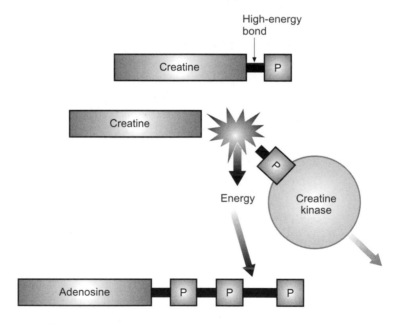

Fig. 5.01 The ATP-PC system.

KEY WORDS

Sarcoplasm

Coupled reaction

Exothermic

Endothermic

Anaerobic

Fuel	Phosphocreatine (PC)
Site of reaction	**Sarcoplasm** (the gel-like content of a muscle cell)
Active enzymes	Creatine kinase
Equations (a **coupled reaction** where the energy released from one reaction is used in the next)	PC = P + C + energy (an **exothermic** reaction which releases energy) energy + ADP + P = ATP (an **endothermic** reaction which requires energy)

ATP yield	1 ATP 2 ATP
By-products	None (phosphate group that can be re-synthesised back to PC)
Advantages	Very quick ATP re-synthesis due to PC being stored in muscle cell and the reaction being anaerobic (not requiring oxygen); well suited to short duration, powerful events
Disadvantages	Only small amount stored therefore limited amount of ATP can be re-synthesised
Threshold	Maximum of 10 seconds

3 The lactic acid system

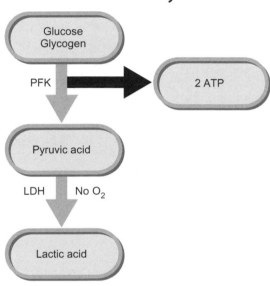

Fig. 5.02 The lactic acid system.

Practical examples	Long jump
Fuel	Glucose (glycogen)
Site of reaction	Sarcoplasm
Active enzymes	Phosphofructokinase (PFK)/Lactatedehydrogenase (LDH)
ATP Yield	2 ATP
By-products	Lactic Acid
Advantages	**Anaerobic glycolysis** (the partial breakdown of glucose to **pyruvic acid**) is a relatively quick system that can provide larger amounts of ATP re-synthesis than PC
Disadvantages	Lactic acid causes local muscle fatigue
Threshold	2–3 minutes (maximum)
Practical examples	400m sprint

KEY WORDS

Anaerobic glycosis

Pyruvic acid

Mitochondria

4 The aerobic system

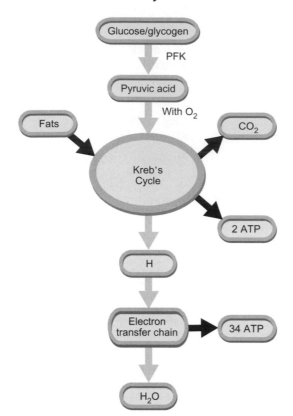

Fig. 5.03 The aerobic system.

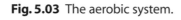

Fuel	Glucose (glycogen) and fats
Site of reaction	Glycolysis – sarcoplasm Kreb's Cycle – mitochondria (matrix) Electron transfer chain – mitochondria (cristae)
Active enzymes	PFK
Equation	$C_6H_{12}O_6 + 6O_2 \rightarrow 6CO_2 + 6H_2O + energy$
ATP yield	36–8 ATP for whole system 2 ATP for glycolysis 2 ATP during Kreb's Cycle 34 ATP during electron transfer chain
By-products	Kreb's Cycle – CO_2 and hydrogen atoms Electron transfer chain – H_2O
Advantages	Large amounts of ATP re-sysnthesis possible for long duration (low intensity) exercise. No harmful by-products
Disadvantages	A large number of chemical reactions plus the need for a large supply of oxygen make this system suitable only for low-intensity exercise
Threshold	Hours
Practical examples	Marathon, triathlon, etc.

5 The energy continuum

The **energy continuum** describes the relative contribution of each of the three energy systems to re-synthesising ATP. This contribution will vary according to the duration and intensity of exercise. It is important to realise that all three energy systems could be used during certain activities. For example, in a game of hockey a short sprint to intercept the ball would predominantly use the ATP-PC system, where a long run down the wing may predominantly use the lactic acid system. Jogging back into position during general play would be an example of the aerobic system's contribution.

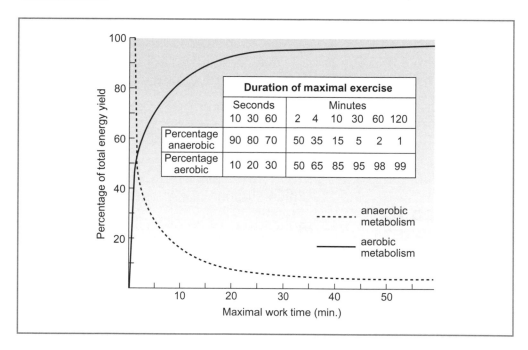

Duration of maximal exercise								
	Seconds			Minutes				
	10	30	60	2	4	10	30	60	120
Percentage anaerobic	90	80	70	50	35	15	5	2	1
Percentage aerobic	10	20	30	50	65	85	95	98	99

Fig. 5.04 The relative contribution of aerobic and anaerobic energy systems to physical activity.

6 Thresholds

The threshold of an energy system is the point at which it can no longer supply energy for the activity. The threshold of each system is included in the energy system tables.

KEY WORDS

OBLA   Onset of blood lactate accumulation (**OBLA**) is the point at which there is a rapid increase in the amount of lactic acid found in the blood. Most performers try to avoid reaching this point as the increase in lactic acid leads to a drop in pH, which inhibits enzyme action and leads to muscle fatigue.

✓ CHECK !

Go back to the overview diagrams on p. 137. If you are satisfied with your knowledge and understanding, tick off the sections that you have revised so far. If you are not satisfied, then revisit those sections and refer to the pages in the 'Need to know more?'

Section 2: *The recovery process*

Section overview

1 Excessive post-exercise oxygen consumption (EPOC)	☐
2 Alactacid debt (the fast stage)	☐
3 Lactacid debt (the slow stage)	☐
4 Removal of CO_2	☐
5 Replenishment of glycogen stores	☐
6 Implications of recovery for planning training sessions	☐

NEED TO KNOW MORE?

For further information on the recovery process, see pp. 279–83 in *Advanced PE for OCR: A2*.

Tick the box when you are satisfied with your level of knowledge and understanding for each topic within this section.

1 Excessive post-exercise oxygen consumption (EPOC)

After exercise, heart rate and ventilation rates remain elevated to help your body recover. The recovery process is required to return the body to its pre-exercise state. Energy is required, provided by the aerobic system, to remove the waste products of exercise and replenish the stores used.

KEY WORDS

EPOC

An excess of oxygen needs to be present and this is known as excessive post-exercise oxygen consumption (**EPOC**). This can be broken down into two components: the alactacid stage and the lactacid stage.

2 Alactacid debt (the fast stage)

During this stage, the energy provided by the elevated metabolism is used to help the ATP-PC system recover and also to restore oxygen levels in the myoglobin.

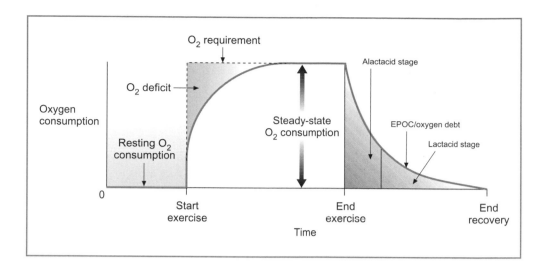

Fig. 5.05 Oxygen consumption during exercise and recovery.

3 Lactacid debt (the slow stage)

During this stage, lactic acid is removed from the body in a number of ways.

	How long?	How much oxygen?
Replace PC stores	180 secs for full recovery	4 litres
Replace oxygen in myoglobin	60–120 secs	0.5 litres
Remove lactic acid by: • converting to CO_2 and H_2O via the aerobic system • converting to glucose/glycogen (Cori Cycle) • converting to protein • removing via sweat and urine	Up to an hour	5–8 litres

4 Removal of CO_2

Carbon dioxide dissolved in blood plasma will reduce pH. This triggers chemoreceptors to stimulate the cardiac and respiratory centres to elevate cardiac output and respiratory rate, thus removing CO_2 via the lungs.

5 Replenishment of glycogen stores

It can take 48 hours to restore the glycogen stores after a prolonged or strenuous event. A high carbohydrate diet is required to maximise these stores.

HOT TIPS

Do not include restoration of glycogen as an answer for a question on EPOC – it does not require excess O2 for its restoration.

NEED TO KNOW MORE?

For further information on OBLA, see p. 277 *Advanced PE for OCR: A2.*

6 Implications of recovery for planning training sessions

Implication	Explanation
Give sufficient recovery time for high intensity/speed work	Takes 3 mins for full PC recovery – quality of speed work will be reduced if insufficient recovery is given
Use an active cool down	Moderate levels of activity during cool down increase the speed of lactic acid removal
Monitor training intensities carefully	Avoid the build up of lactic acid in the first place
Warm up thoroughly	Will reduce the amount of oxygen deficit at the start of exercise

 CHECK !

Go back to the overview diagrams on pp. 137 and 142. If you are satisfied with your knowledge and understanding, tick off the sections that you have revised so far. If you are not satisfied, then revisit those sections and refer to the pages in the 'Need to know more?'

Section 3: *Principles of training*

Section overview

1 The six principles ☐
2 Physiological implications of the warm-up ☐
3 Delayed onset of muscle soreness (DOMS) ☐
4 Physiological implications of a cool down ☐
5 Periodisation of training ☐

NEED TO KNOW MORE?

For further information on the principles of training, see pp. 284–9 in *Advanced PE for OCR: A2.*

Tick the box when you are satisfied with your level of knowledge and understanding for each topic within this section.

HOT TIPS

Make sure you can give a practical example for each of the six principles.

1 The six principles

Certain rules govern the use of all training methods and these are known as the principles of training. You need to understand and be able to apply six of them.

Principle	Description	Practical Application
Specificity	Relevant to the individual and the activity	Relevant to the: • energy system/fitness component • muscle group • movement pattern
Progression	As the body adapts, further increases in overload must occur	Make progression gradual
Overload (FIT)	Make the body work harder than usual	Increase frequency Increase intensity Increase time/duration
Reversibility	When training stops, adaptations are lost	Maintain some training during holidays, injury, out of season
Moderation	Over-training could lead to injury	Make progressive overload gradual to avoid injury
Variance	Use a variety of training types	Maintains motivation Avoids overuse injuries

2 Physiological implications of the warm-up

A warm-up routine helps prepare the body for the forthcoming exercise. You need to know what physiological responses occur during warm up and what advantages these may give to the performer.

Muscular	
Implication	*Explanation*
Reduction of injury	Greater elasticity of muscle
Greater speed and strength of contraction	Greater elasticity of muscle Better co-ordination of antagonistic pairs

Cardio-vascular	
Implication	*Explanation*
Increased enzyme activity	Increased temperature
Increased cardiac output	Greater venous return from working muscles
Increased blood flow to working muscles	Vasoconstriction and vasodilation (vascular shunt mechanism)
Prevention of OBLA	Increased blood flow

KEY WORDS

DOMS

3 Delayed onset of muscle soreness (DOMS)

DOMS is the muscle soreness you feel 24 to 48 hours after a training period/competition. It is caused by damage to the muscle fibres, particularly during eccentric contractions.

To prevent DOMS:

HOT TIPS

Remember, DOMS occurs 24–48 hours after exercise and is caused by muscle damage not lactic acid.

- warm up thoroughly
- avoid eccentric work at the start of a training session
- apply the principles of progression, moderation and variance to your training.

To reduce the effects of DOMS, use:

- massage
- hot baths
- ice therapy.

4 Physiological implications of a cool down

The main benefits of a cool down are to speed up the recovery process.

Muscular	
Implication	*Explanation*
Prevention of muscle damage	Allows the muscle to cool down slowly not suddenly
Good time for flexibility work	Muscle is already warm and elastic

Cardio-vascular	
Implication	*Explanation*
Removal of lactic acid	Increased blood flow helps to metabolise lactic acid
Removal of CO_2	Increased blood flow helps to remove CO_2 via the lungs
Prevention of blood pooling	Maintains venous return by the action of the muscle pump

KEY WORDS

Periodisation

5 Periodisation of training

The aim of training is to improve performance, often for a specific event. The process of breaking down the training programme into manageable sections, each with its own goal, is known as **periodisation**.

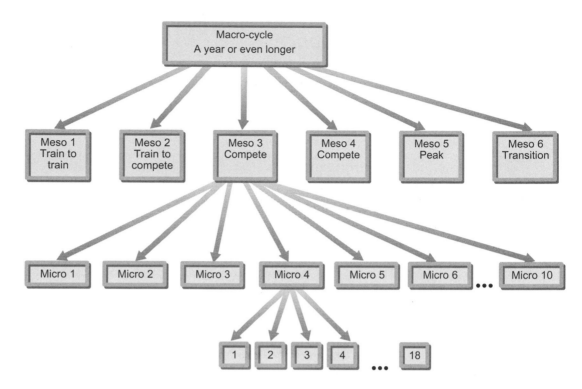

Fig. 5.06 The training programme.

KEY WORDS

Macro-cycle

Meso-cycle

Micro-cycle

Units

The whole programme with its main aim of success at a specific event is known as the **macro-cycle**. This is often a year but can be longer, such as a four-year plan for an Olympic athlete.

This large cycle is split into smaller blocks of maybe 4 or 6 weeks, known as a **meso-cycle**. The number of these will vary according to the athlete and the nature of the activity, but often a year will include 5 or 6 mesocycles to cover preparation, competition and recovery (sometimes known as transition).

HOT TIPS

Make sure you know how to structure units throughout the micro-cycle using principles of training.

Each mesocycle is divided into **micro-cycles**, which are often the training week. Each of these weeks is split into **units**, and sometimes as many as 18 units are completed in any one week. Each unit has a specific aim. For example, you may do a unit on speed, one on flexibility, another on upper body strength, and so on. A typical training session may contain a number of different units.

NEED TO KNOW MORE?

For further information on periodisation, see pp. 287–8 in *Advanced PE for OCR: A2*.

✔ CHECK !

Go back to the overview diagrams on pp. 137 and 144. If you are satisfied with your knowledge and understanding, tick off the sections that you have revised so far. If you are not satisfied, then revisit those sections and refer to the pages in the 'Need to know more?'

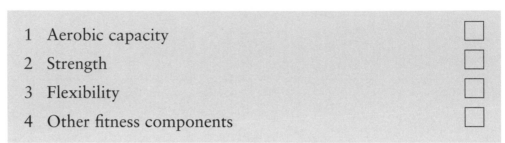

Section 4: *Components of fitness and improving performance*

Section overview

NEED TO KNOW MORE?

For further information on components of fitness and improving performance, see pp. 290–306 in *Advanced PE for OCR: A2*

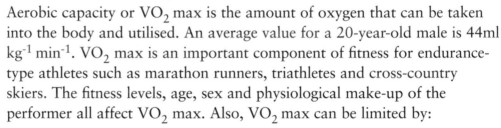

1 Aerobic capacity ☐

2 Strength ☐

3 Flexibility ☐

4 Other fitness components ☐

Tick the box when you are satisfied with your level of knowledge and understanding for each topic within this section.

1 Aerobic capacity

HOT TIPS

For each fitness component in this book, know the name of a test, brief methodology and how the result is evaluated. Often 'compare to standardised table' will secure a mark!

Aerobic capacity or VO₂ max is the amount of oxygen that can be taken into the body and utilised. An average value for a 20-year-old male is 44ml kg⁻¹ min⁻¹. VO_2 max is an important component of fitness for endurance-type athletes such as marathon runners, triathletes and cross-country skiers. The fitness levels, age, sex and physiological make-up of the performer all affect VO_2 max. Also, VO_2 max can be limited by:

- external respiration – the amount of oxygen entering our bodies
- transport of oxygen around the body – the capacity of the blood to carry oxygen and the ability of the heart to pump it to the working muscles
- internal respiration – the removal of oxygen from the blood into the muscle cell
- utilisation of oxygen – how well our muscles can use the oxygen once it has reached the muscle cell.

A number of tests are available for measuring VO_2 max, some maximal, others predictors from sub-maximal readings. The most common test is the multistage fitness test. Performers complete a progressive and maximal 20m shuttle run test and compare their final stage score with standard tables provided with the test.

There are three main methods of aerobic training:

HOT TIPS

Remember to use FIT.
For Aerobic training:
- **F** = 3–5 days a week
- **I** = 55–90% maximal heart rate
- **T** = 20–60 minutes of continuous or intermittent exercise.

Continuous training	Training at a steady intensity – approximately 70% of maximum heart rate for at least 30 minutes
Fartlek training	Continuous running training but with elements of varied pace, terrain and incline. Can help replicate and simulate game situation and prevents boredom
Interval training	Periods of work divided by periods of rest/recovery. The intensity of the session can be controlled by manipulating the: • work period • rest period • intensity of work period • activity of rest period • number of sets and repetitions • work : relief ratio

NEED TO KNOW MORE?

For further information on the adaptations, see pp. 294–5 in *Advanced PE for OCR: A2*.

After a period of aerobic training lasting approximately 12 weeks, the following long-term adaptations will have occurred.

KEY WORDS

Hypertrophy

Area	Adaptation	Effect
Lungs	• Respiratory muscles get stronger • Lung volume increases • Maximum pulmonary ventilation increases	• Greater gas exchange
Heart	• Myocardial **hypertrophy** (increase in the size of the heart muscle) • Resting heart rate decreases	• Stroke volume increases • Heart becomes more efficient
Vascular system	• Arterial walls become more elastic • Increased number of capillaries at muscles and lungs • Blood plasma volume increases • Red blood cells and haemoglobin increase	• Maintains and increases blood flow to muscles • Increased amount of oxygen reaching muscle
Muscle	• Mitochondria increase in size and number • Increase in enzyme activity • Increase in muscle glycogen stores • Myoglobin levels increase	• Increase aerobic metabolism • More oxygen to mitochondria

HOT TIPS

Make sure you can explain the benefits of these adaptations.

The aerobic energy system is the key provider of energy for this fitness component but remember that energy systems do not work in complete isolation from the others (see the energy continuum on pp. 140–1 of this book). There will be times, even in a marathon, where the performer needs some help from anaerobic systems.

2 Strength

There are three different types of strength.

Type of strength	Definition	Example
Maximal strength	The maximum force that can be exerted by a muscle in one single contraction	Weightlifting
Explosive strength	The ability to overcome resistance with a high speed of contraction	Shot put
Strength endurance	The ability to sustain a number of muscular contractions for a period of time	Olympic rowing

Each type of strength needs a specific test. An example of each type is given below.

Maximal strength	Hand grip dynamometer
Explosive strength	Sergeant jump/Wingate test
Strength endurance	Sports Coach UK sit-up test

The strength of a muscle will be determined by the following two factors.

• Muscle fibre type	Type IIb fibres provide the strongest force of contraction
• Cross-sectional area	The greater the cross-sectional size, the greater the force of contraction

Training strength requires some form of resistance. This can be provided by weights, both machine and free; body resistance, as in a press-up; and other devices, such as bungee cords and parachutes. For each type of strength, the manipulation of overload is achieved through three components.

Repetitions	The number of times the exercise is to be performed without stopping
Sets	A specified number of repetitions of an exercise followed by a period of rest (at least for that muscle group)
Resistance (repetition maximum)	The maximum load a muscle group can lift a given number of times without fatiguing. For example, a ten repetition maximum or 10RM is the weight or load a person can lift ten times and ten times only

These three components are manipulated differently for each type of strength.

Maximal strength	• Resistance training Frequency: at least twice a week Intensity: 80+% of maximum (1RM) Time: 3 sets of 1–7 reps • Circuit training – a series of 8–10 exercises where performers usually work for a period of time before rotating to the next station
Explosive strength	• Resistance training Frequency: at least twice a week Intensity: 40–75% of maximum (1RM) Time: 3 sets of 6–10 reps • Plyometrics – exercises that rely on a mixture of eccentric and concentric muscle contractions to develop strength; for example, double-footed hurdle jumps • Circuit training • Interval training
Strength endurance	• Resistance training Frequency: at least twice a week Intensity: 40–80% of maximum (1RM) Time: 4–6 sets of 12+ reps • Circuit training • Interval training

NEED TO KNOW MORE?

For further information on strength training, see pp. 296–301 in *Advanced PE for OCR: A2*.

Adaptations occur after about eight weeks of strength training and include changes to the muscle cells and the neural system that controls them.

Muscle cells	• Muscle hypertrophy (including **hyperplasia** – the splitting of fibres to create new ones) • Increase in ATP stores • Increase in phosphocreatine stores • Increase in glycogen stores
Neural system	• Increased recruitment of motor units • Better synchronisation of motor units

KEY WORDS

Hyperplasia

The energy system predominantly used changes for each type of strength.

Maximal strength	ATP/PC system
Explosive strength	ATP/PC system
Strength endurance	ATP/PC and lactic acid system

3 Flexibility

There are two types of flexibility.

NEED TO KNOW MORE?

For further information on flexibility , see pp. 301–4 in *Advanced PE for OCR: A2*.

Type of flexibility	Definition	Example
Static flexibility	The maximum range of movement at a joint with no emphasis on the speed of movement	The splits in gymnastics
Dynamic flexibility	The ability to use a range of movement at a joint in the performance of a physical activity	High hurdle technique

Due to the specific nature of flexibility, individual tests are required for each area of the body. A commonly used test is the sit and reach test. There are numerous other tests for other regions of the body and many use equipment called goniometers to measure the angle at a joint.

Flexibility is very specific as there are a large number of factors that affect the range of movement at a joint. These include:

- type of joint, for example ball-and-socket is usually the most flexible type of joint
- shape of the bones
- length and elasticity of muscle tissue
- length of tendons and ligaments
- elasticity of skin and amount of fat around joint
- temperature of all soft tissue
- age and sex of performer.

KEY WORDS

Active stretches

Passive stretches

PNF

Three main training techniques are used for the development of flexibility:

- static stretches – **active stretches** and **passive stretches**
- ballistic stretching
- proprioceptive neuromuscular facilitation (**PNF**).

Static stretches

Static stretches are traditional stretches, such as the adapted hamstring stretch, where the position is held for 10–30 seconds. The performer can create the stretch by actively moving into the stretch position (an active stretch), or they can allow a partner to move a joint through the range of movement for them (a passive stretch).

Ballistic stretching

This type of stretch involves a dynamic movement to move the joint to the end of its range of movement. Performers must make sure they are adequately warmed up and flexible before using these techniques.

Proprioceptive neuromuscular facilitation (PNF)

This technique relies on the process of reciprocal innervation to allow a muscle to stretch further. A static stretch is performed, followed by an isometric contraction and a further static stretch. Often the second stretch will allow a greater range of movement.

Remember to apply the FIT principle to all flexibility training.

Frequency	2–3 times a week
Intensity	Mild tension but no pain
Time	Hold each stretch for 10–30 seconds and repeat 3–5 times

4 Other fitness components

	Definition	Test
Body composition	The percentage of muscle fat and bone in the body	Skin fold callipers (Jackson and Pollock) or hydrostatic weighing
Balance	The ability to maintain the centre of mass above the base of support; can be static (handstand) or dynamic (landing after catching a netball)	Stork balance
Co-ordination	The ability to put a number of body systems into action simultaneously, e.g. hand and eyes	Ball toss test
Agility	The ability to change body position in a precise and balanced manner	Illinois agility run
Reaction time	The length of time between the reception of a stimulus and the initiation of a response	Ruler drop test, various computer time reaction tests
Speed	The ability to move body parts quickly	Rolling 30m sprint

 CHECK!

Go back to the overview diagrams on pp. 137 and 148. If you are satisfied with your knowledge and understanding, tick off the sections that you have revised so far. If you are not satisfied, then revisit those sections and refer to the pages in the 'Need to know more?'

Section 5: *Ergogenic aids*

Section overview

NEED TO KNOW MORE?

For further information on ergogenic aids, see pp. 306–12 in *Advanced PE for OCR: A2*.

1 Nutritional aids   ☐

2 Other aids to performance   ☐

Tick the box when you are satisfied with your level of knowledge and understanding for each topic within this section.

An ergogenic aid is any substance or object that helps performance. Although the list is almost endless, you are required to know about the following.

1 Nutritional aids

Aid	Method	Positive effects	Negative effects	Who would benefit?
Carbo-loading	• 7 days before competition – deplete glycogen stores by heavy training and low carbohydrate diet • 3 days before competition – reduce training and eat carbohydrate-rich diet to replace stores • Body 'super-compensates' and stores more glycogen than before	Increased glycogen stores in muscles and liver	• Quality of training may be poor due to lack of carbohydrate in run up to competition • Danger of having depleted glycogen stores if correct diet is not followed prior to competition • Weight gain due to water retention	Performers taking part in long duration aerobic events – for example, marathon runners
Pre-event meals	• High-carbohydrate meals should be eaten 3/4 days before competition to maintain muscle glycogen stores • High-carbohydrate meal should be eaten 2–4 hours before to maintain liver glycogen levels • Glucose can be eaten just prior to exercise (5 mins) if the athlete is comfortable doing so	Increased glycogen stores in muscles and liver	Glucose eaten 15–45 minutes before exercise can have a detrimental effect, causing insulin to convert blood glucose to liver glycogen, which results in temporary hypoglycaemia	Games players and any aerobic athlete
Post-event meals	• Best time to replace glycogen stores is immediately after exercise (within 2 hours) • It can take 48 hours to replace fully	High glycogen stores for following training/ competition	None	Any performer using glycogen as a fuel

2 Other aids to performance

Aid	Method	Positive effects	Negative effects	Who would benefit?
Creatine supplements	Powder/fluid supplement	Increases the amount of phosphocreatine stored in the muscle	• Can put strain on organs such as the liver • Possible chance of increasing dehydration in performers	High intensity athletes such as 100m sprinters
Blood doping	• Remove red blood cells and store • Train as normal for five weeks • Reinfuse red blood cells prior to event	Increase in red blood cells/haemoglobin, which increases oxygen to working muscles	Danger of blood clotting, heart failure and contamination	All endurance athletes
Rh EPO	EPO is a hormone that stimulates red blood cell production	As above	Same as above but without the risk of contamination	As above
Nasal strips	Elastic strip to increase amount of air entering the lungs	None	None	No one
Caffeine	Increase caffeine intake prior to event using concentrated caffeine products	Caffeine improves alertness, concentration and reaction time and also fat metabolism during aerobic metabolism	Nervousness, anxiety, sleep deprivation, dehydration and addiction	Generally endurance athletes for the benefits to fat metabolism
Alcohol	Consume alcohol before competition	None, although performer may feel more relaxed and confident	Dehydration and impairment of psychomotor performance	No one
Hormones and anabolic steroids	Use of steroid-based substances such as Nandrolone and hormone treatments such as HGH (human growth hormone)	Increase muscle mass and strength; maybe help with recovery from high-intensity training	• Increased aggression, androgenic effects such as breast development, facial hair . • HGH can cause dangerous organ enlargement and deformity of the bones.; • Diabetes and high blood pressure	High-intensity power athletes such as weightlifters and sprinters

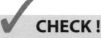 **CHECK !**

Go back to the overview diagrams on pp. 136, 137 and 153. If you are satisfied with your knowledge and understanding, tick off the sections that you have revised so far. If you are not satisfied, then revisit those sections and refer to the pages in the 'Need to know more?'

Exam practice

1 Provide the missing information A, B and C from the table below.

Predominant energy System	Fuel used	Active enzyme	Site(s) of reaction
ATP-PC	PC	Creatine Kinase	B
Aerobic	Glycogen and fats	A	C

(3 marks)

2 The graph below shows the relationship of the energy systems utilised over a one-mile race by a top-class performer.

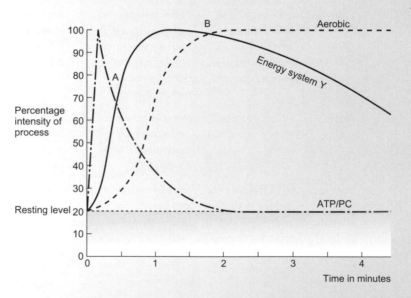

Identify energy system Y and outline the physiological processes occurring in the body between points A and B on the graph. **(3 marks)**

3 Some games activities rely heavily on anaerobic energy systems. Using examples from physical education or sport, show how knowledge of the recovery process can be put into practice to the athlete's advantage.

(3 marks)

4   The coach is responsible for ensuring the performer is in peak condition as competition approaches. Using three principles of training, explain how this will be achieved in a named activity.   **(6 marks)**

5   Define aerobic capacity and maximal strength and identify a test that could be used to evaluate each of these components.   **(4 marks)**

6   Aerobic capacity is important for endurance athletes such as triathletes to enable them to work at a higher percentage of their VO_2 max before they reach OBLA.

The table below compares VO_2 max and OBLA values for two 18-year-old students. One is a top-club triathlete and the other a reasonable school team tennis player.

	VO_2max (ml kg^{-1} min^{-1})	OBLA (as a % of VO_2 max)
Triathlete	57	80%
Tennis player	34	50%

With reference to the efficiency of the vascular system, explain why the triathlete is able to achieve these higher values.   **(5 marks)**

7   Describe the types of training that can be used to increase the range of movement in a joint. (Adapted question)   **(4 marks)**

8   Agility, balance, co-ordination, reaction time and speed are components of skill-related fitness. Define two of these components and identify a recognised test for each. (Adapted question)   **(4 marks)**

9   For some endurance athletes, the pressure to perform at the highest level means that the temptation to gain unfair aerobic training benefits from ergogenic aids, despite the dangers, becomes too great. Outline how a named physiological (not nutritional) aid would benefit such an athlete and identify the health risks associated with it.   **(4 marks)**

10   Define the term 'carbo-loading', explain how it is achieved and give an example of the type of athlete who would benefit most from this practice.   **(4 marks)**

Now go to page 182 to check your answers.

Unit 6: The improvement of effective performance and critical evaluation of the practical activities with synoptic application

Unit Overview

Chapter 6: Synoptic application	☐

Tick the box when you are satisfied with your level of knowledge and understanding for this chapter.

Chapter 6: **Synoptic application**

Chapter Overview

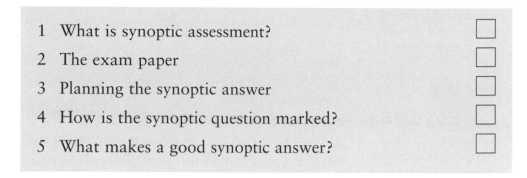

1 What is synoptic assessment?

2 The exam paper

3 Planning the synoptic answer

4 How is the synoptic question marked?

5 What makes a good synoptic answer?

NEED TO KNOW MORE?

For further information on synoptic assessment, see pp. 331–43 in *Advanced PE for OCR: A2*.

Tick the box when you are satisfied with your level of knowledge and understanding for each topic within this chapter.

1 What is synoptic assessment?

HOT TIPS

PE (OCR) is different from many other subjects in terms of synoptic assessment in that it does not require integration of the whole course in the written answer.

For each A level course, the approach to, and assessment of, the synoptic element is different. The aim of synoptic assessment is to test overall understanding of the course at the end – that is, both AS and A2 work. For synoptic assessment of PE (OCR), you are required to:

- demonstrate an integrated understanding of the course during your oral evaluation and appreciation of practical performance (5% of your final mark)
- write an extended answer showing knowledge and understanding as well as relationships within and between one AS area and one A2 area that you have studied (15% of your final mark).

2 The exam paper

- The exam paper containing the synoptic questions will comprise a multi-page booklet.
- The compulsory Exercise and sport physiology question forms Section A of the same paper.
- The synoptic questions form Section B.
- The exam is 1½ hours long.
- No longer than 30 minutes should be spent on Section A.
- Approximately one hour should therefore be spent on Section B.
- You will answer one synoptic question.
- The question will be either scientific or socio-cultural.

- The question will have two parts:
  - Part 1 will examine AS work (and may have up to three sub-sections within it).
  - Part 2 will examine A2 work. (and may have up to three sub-sections within it).
- You need to choose whether to answer a scientific or socio-cultural question.
- If you choose scientific, you have to choose whether to do scientific/physiological or scientific/psychological, or whether you wish to combine the two (for example, Anatomy and physiology for AS and Sport psychology for A2).
- If you choose socio-cultural (but only if you have studied both the historical and comparative options), you need to choose between them for your Part 2 (A2) part question.
- The diagram below shows all the possible question routes.

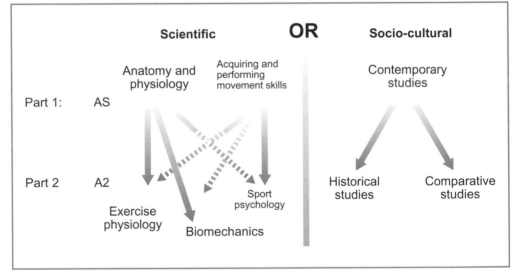

Fig. 6.01 Possible question/answer routes

- The solid arrows in Figure 6.01 should give more scope for making links between AS and A2 work.
- The dashed arrows (which combine physiological and psychological work), are allowed by the rubric of the examination, but will give inferior opportunity for making links between AS and A2. However, these options need not be dismissed if your knowledge of the questions is very good.

3 Planning the synoptic answer

- To score well on this important part of your PE exam, you must plan your answer.
- Spend time before the examination practising planning answers for past questions to find a style that suits you.

HOT TIPS

Use past papers to find your own planning style.

The one-hour allowed for the synoptic question might be divided as follows:

15 minutes	Choosing question and planning answer
20 minutes	Writing up Part 1 (AS)
20 minutes	Writing up Part 2 (A2)
5 minutes	Proofreading/checking your answer.

Your plan should not be over-elaborate or you could run out of time when writing up your answer.

Here is a possible planning grid and the order in which some students might approach their synoptic answer.

HOT TIPS

Remember, only one full question should be answered: Part 1 (AS) plus Part 2 (A2).

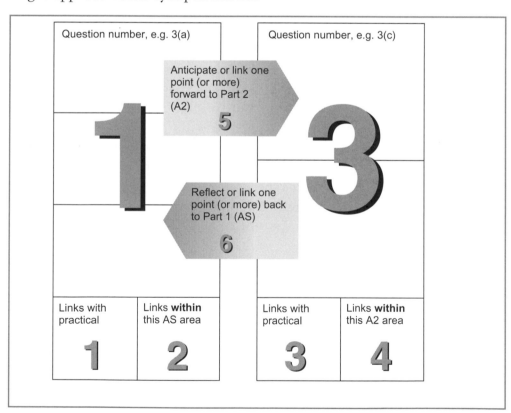

Fig. 6.02 A possible planning grid and order for the synoptic answer.

These are some examples of planned questions:

The scientific question: question 2

The physiological route

This is a question about performance in sport being best served if the coach has an understanding of sport science. A candidate should use their knowledge and experience in a specific sport when answering this question.

- Part 1 (AS)

  Analyse the movement of either the shoulder or the hip joint in a named skill selected from a sport of your choice.

  Explain the physiological effects of a warm-up on skeletal muscle tissue.

- Part 2 (A2)

  The coach is responsible for ensuring the performer is in peak condition as a competition approaches. Using principles of training, explain how this will be achieved in a named activity.

  See p. 163 for a possible answer plan.

The scientific question: question 2

The psychological route

- Part 1 (AS)

  Describe how information is processed in order to produce a skilful performance.

  Explain how an understanding of information processing can help the teaching of sports skills.

- Part 2 (A2)

  Explain why the degree of arousal experienced by a performer will increase the quality of performance in a sports situation.

  Outline the strategies that could be used by the coach to control the athlete's concentration during a sports event.

  See p. 163 for a possible answer plan.

The socio-cultural question: question 3

This is a question about mass participation and is for a student who chooses the comparative rather than the historical route at A2.

- Part 1 (AS)

  What factors might affect a person's opportunity to take part in regular physical activity in the UK? Give brief explanations for each point that you make.

- Part 2 (A2)

  How has France encouraged mass participation in sport and outdoor activities?

  With reference to cultural factors, discuss how opportunities differ between France and the UK for taking part in sport and outdoor activities.

Question 2, Part 1 (AS – Anatomy and Physiology)

Joint movement analysis
Shoulder:
- Ball and socket.
- Head of Humorous and Glenoid Cavity of Scapula.
- Freely moveable.
- (Flexion/extension/horizontal flexion/horizontal extension).
- (Abduction/adduction/circumduction/rotation).
- Antagonistic muscle action.

Effects of a warm-up on skeletal muscle tissue
- Reduced Injury risk.
- Increased flexibility/elasticity.
- Increased blood flow to muscles.
- Increased speed of nerve impulses.
- Decreased possibility of DOMS.
- Delays OBLA.
- Increased enzyme action.
- Improved co-ordination between antagonistic pairs (reciprocal innervation).

Question 2, Part 2 (A2 – Exercise and Sport Physiology)

Principles of training
- Specificity: relevant to netball and individual player (shooter).
- Overload: work harder than usual by increasing frequency/intensity/time.
- Progression/moderation: take things gradually/avoid injury, e.g. progressive overload.
- Variance: vary training to relieve boredom, e.g. ensure that training takes a number of different forms.
- Reversibility: training must be continuous otherwise benefits are reversed, e.g. avoid long breaks in training at important times as adaptations can be reversed and benefits decreased.
- Periodisation: training in bocks depending on the season, e.g. during out-of-season phase, netball player must keep a good level of general fitness; pre-season she will build more specific fitness; during competitive season she will reinforce match fitness.

Warm-up would also include skill practices specific to netball. Progression and moderation both work to reduce the risk of injury, as does a warm-up.

Shooter in netball: importance of skill practices in warm-up - throwing, catching, shooting. Warm-up and cool down sometimes included as a principle of training.

HOT TIPS

Just mentioning a sport is not usually enough to gain credit for a practical link. It must be specific and applied.

Links with practical
- Shooting in netball (execution phase):
- Shoulder flexion.
- Agonist = anterior deltoid.
- Concentric contraction.
- Antagonist = posterior deltoid.
- Relaxes.
- Fixator = pectoralis major
- Isometric contraction
- Warm-up important due to high-intensity activity from the start.
- Need quick reaction, therefore speed of nerve impulse important.

*Links **within** this AS area*
- Structure of ball and socket joint.
- Muscle fibre types and netball shooter.
- Heart rate and netball shooter.

Links with practical

Specificity:
- Work the ATP-PC energy system.
- Improve leg/arm strength and shoulder flexibility.
- Practise throwing/catching/ shooting skills.

Overload:
- Training sessions to occur more often each week.
- Training sessions to be more demanding so shooter works at a higher percentage of her maximum heart rate.
- Training sessions to last for a longer time.

*Links **within** this A2 area*
- Health-related fitness components: aerobic capacity, muscular, flexibility.
- Skill-related fitness components: dynamic balance, co-ordination, ability, RT, speed.
- Recovery: alactacid component.
- Interval training.

Fig 6.03 The scientific question (Physiological – Anatomy and Physiology to Exercise and Sport Physiology route): possible answer plan.

Question 2, Part 1 (AS – Acquiring and Performing Movement Skills)

Information processing for skilful performance
- Input, e.g. all information when receiving serve in tennis.
- Detection, e.g. vision, audition and kineasthsis relating to receiving the tennis serve.
- Perception operates in STM, e.g. speed, direction and angle of the serve.
- Selective attention operates within STM, e.g. focus directly on flight of ball.
- Cognition, e.g. a decision to play a forehand drive to return serve.
- Translatory mechanism effector.
- Feedback, e.g. preparation backswing feels right.
- Feedback, e.g. forehand drive was successful.

Teaching of sports skills
- Overload, e.g. during demonstration of the drive stroke.
- Mental rehearsal, e.g. visualise the pattern of movement.
- Selective attention: consider the perceptual requirements, e.g. forehand drive is an open skill requiring a varied practice.
- Practice conditions, e.g. lower the net/short tennis/restrict court.
- Guidance, e.g. target to hit.
- Transfer.
- Cognition, e.g. lack of understanding.
- Motor output, e.g. faulty output.
- Feedback.

Question 2, Part 2 (A2 – Psychology of Sport Performance)

Degree of arousal
- Information processing: the degree of arousal determines the effectiveness of information processing, e.g. speed and accuracy of decision.
- Drive theory.
- Inverted U theory.
- Perceptual adjustment
- ZOF.
- Peak flow.
- Attentional styles.

Control of concentration
- Stress management: desensitasation. e.g. control stress prior to an important event
- Cognitive visualisation. e.g. rehearse the skill mentally, for example by imagining a successful goal kick
- Self-efficacy.
- Selective attention - tell the athletes what to expect
- Attribution. Attribute success to ability and effort in specific skill
- Goal-setting - follow principles of SMARTER targets in specific skill
- Perception: ensure a balanced/realistic perception between ability and task.
- Skill learning.
- Teamwork/cohesion.
- Accountability: reduce the amount of individual accountability.

Arousal level influences the speed and accuracy of decision making. Learning is best achieved in conditions of low arousal.

Attention is improved if the athlete is in a situation which involves their strongest style. Repetitive practice grooves the skill to produce a dominant response. Coaches should be aware of problem of Drive Reduction.

HOT TIPS

It is often more straightforward to think of linking comments within a subject area than between AS and A2 subject areas.

Links with practical

See examples above.

*Links **within** this AS area*
- Decision through varied practice.
- Information processing and reaction time.
- Mental rehearsal.
- Decision making.
- Operant conditioning.

Links with practical

See examples above.

*Links **within** this A2 area*
- Optimal arousal differs according to personality, task type, experience and stage of learning.
- Optimal arousal allows access to four attentional styles.
- Cognitive visualisation.
- Self-efficacy theory (Bandura) raises specific self-confidence.
- Sports confidence theory (Vealey) raises trait confidence.

Fig 6.04 The scientific question (psychological route): possible answer plan.

Question 3, Part 1 (AS – Contemporary Studies)

Factors affecting participation
- Gender: more men take part than women (suggest why).
- Ability: you may not be good enough to join a private club.
- Disability: you may lack self-esteem (comment on Tani Gray as role model who has improved situation).
- Age: you may be put off by your experiences at school.
- Money: you may have a low disposable income.
- School: you may have poor facilities.
- Friends/peer pressure: your friends' interests are likely to affect your own interests and activities.

Question 3, Part 2 (A2 – Comparative Studies)

Mass participation in France
- *Sport pour tous*.
- Government investment.
- Emphasis on joint provision of facilities.
- Influence of the UNSS.
- Impact of primary sport schools.
- *Les Classes Transplantées*.
- Outward Bound opportunities.

Cultural factor	France	UK
Politics	Heavy investment in sport	Limited investment in sport
Schools/ education	Influence of UNSS, which helps participation as well as excellence	Sport in state schools suffering from several constraints, e.g. funding, staffing, sale of fields
Geography	• France 2½ times size of the UK • Rural	• Small island/large population • Urban
Climate	Variety of climatic types to give more and different opportunities for outdoor activities	The climate of the UK not particularly suitable for outdoor activities
Topography	Mountain ranges allow easy access to skiing	Very limited opportunities for winter activities

Included in A2 question.

- Both Britain and France have a Sport for All policy.
- In all of the focus countries, the constraints on participation are the same.

Links with practical
- If you have enough money you can buy your own equipment and join a private club, e.g. a local tennis club costing £100+ a year.
- Comment on class and tennis clubs, referring to your own experience.

*Links **within** this AS area*
- The more factors that affect someone, the less likely they are to participate.
- Influence of media on participation, e.g. during Wimbledon fortnight.

Links with practical
- School offers many chances to participate, e.g. being taken from Cherbourg in the north to Chamonix in the south for three-week *Classe de Neige*.

*Links **within** this A2 area*
- Comment on opportunities for outdoor recreation and education in Australia.
- Comment on opportunities for outdoor recreation and education in USA.
- Mention the USA's culture of watching rather than participating.
- Mention the passion for sport in Australia – link briefly with cultural factors such as desirable climate/ the need for Australia to find cohesive activities when a new nation.
- Role of women in Britain and changing social attitudes – slower to change in Australia because of cultural background.
- Convict settlers predominantly male and frontierism demanded masculinity/strength/ courage, so women were regarded as inferior for a long time – situation now improving.

HOT TIPS

Links within the A2 comparative area can be made with any country in the syllabus.

HOT TIPS

Remember that for the synoptic question, your comparative answer will require comparisons to be made between the focus country/ countries and the UK.

You may also be able to make comparisons between focus countries.

Fig 6.05 The socio-cultural question (Contemporary to Comparative route): possible answer plan.

See p. 164 for a possible answer plan.

4 How is the synoptic question marked?

- The synoptic question has 45 marks.
- 26 of the 45 marks are awarded for subject-specific knowledge.
- 19 of the 45 marks are awarded for 'synoptic skills'.

What are synoptic skills?

Making a link between • AS and A2 • A2 and AS • within AS • within A2 theory and practical	Analysis	Evaluation	The ability to argue a point or see both sides of an argument
Evidence of independent thought and opinion	Making sound judgements	Using specialist technical vocabulary accurately and consistently	Constructing the answer well and writing fluently with good spelling, punctuation and grammar

5 What makes a good synoptic answer?

- An introduction that shows that the question has been understood.
- Regular practical examples.
- Internal links within Part 1 (AS).
- Internal links within Part 2 (A2).
- At least one link from AS to A2 or vice versa.
- Evidence of personal opinion or judgement (particularly in the socio-cultural question).
- Consistent and accurate use of technical language (particularly in the scientific question).
- Paragraphs that have a clear point and purpose.
- Good quality of written communication.
- All sub-questions in Part 1 (AS) and Part 2 (A2) answered.

Some do's and don'ts

Do	Don't
Do revise your AS work well	Don't worry – the synoptic question for PE is more straightforward than it first appears!
Do just one question (with an AS part and an A2 part)	Don't answer more than one question.
Do either a scientific or a socio-cultural question	Don't combine a scientific and a socio-cultural question
Do stick to what you have studied	Don't attempt questions on routes that you have not studied

HOT TIPS

Imagine the examiner marking your work twice. Firstly (in the normal way) for knowledge, and secondly for synoptic skills such as analysis, evaluation, connections within and between the two areas being written about, judgement, use of specialist vocabulary and quality of written communication.

HOT TIPS

Some questions will be broad and there will be just one part for the full 13 knowledge marks. Others will have sub-sections, which together make up the 13 knowledge marks for AS or the 13 knowledge marks for A2.

HOT TIPS

A high mark will be gained by thinking, selecting and adapting information and for showing skills of integration, analysis, explanation and evaluation.

HOT TIPS

Aim for precise, clear, strong linking statements rather than long-winded, vague or elaborate ones.

Do	Don't
Do focus on knowledge (26 marks out of 45)	Don't be vague or go off the point
Do also focus on 'synoptic' skills, especially linking, analysis, judgement, use of specialist vocabulary and good quality written communication (19 marks out of 45)	Don't restrict your AS revision to one area – you may not like the question that comes up in that area
Do plan your answer with key words and bullet points – remember key words will get you marks!	Don't over-plan! You may run out of time to write up the question
Do take care to answer all sub-parts of the AS question and all sub-parts of the A2 question	Don't write down all the information you can recall without specific reference to the question
Do answer the AS question first and then the A2 question	Don't try to merge the two parts into one essay-style answer

 CHECK !

Go back to the overview diagrams on pp. 158 and 159. If you are satisfied with your knowledge and understanding, tick off the sections that you have revised so far. If you are not satisfied, then revisit those sections and refer to the pages in the 'Need to know more?'

Exam practice

For examples of exam practice questions, see pp. 342–3 of *Advanced PE for OCR: A2.*

Answers to exam practice questions

You can see how you have done in all of the units you have studied by checking your answers here.

 How did you do?

0–16 marks: Urgent! Spend more time on this section and try again.

17–24 marks: Not bad! Review the areas where you lost marks.

25–32 marks: Great! Review the areas where you lost marks.

33–40 marks: Fantastic! Go on!

Unit 4 Physical Education: historical, comparative, biomechanical and sport psychology

Chapter 1 Historical studies

1   2 marks

2 marks for two from:

(must have characteristic and reflection of society for 1 mark)

Characteristic	Reflection of society
Local	Due to lack of transport/poor communications
Unwritten rules	Due to illiteracy/no national governing bodies of sport
Cruel/violent	Due to relatively uncivilised nature of pre-industrial Britain/rough life of labourer/life was cheap/life was harsh
Occasional	Because they took place at annual feasts/fairs/holy days/wakes/no leagues or organised competitions/part of rural calendar
Rural	Because effects of industrial/urban revolutions not yet felt/pre-industrial
Wagering	Because wagering was widespread/fashionable/rags to riches

2   4 marks

4 marks for four from:

(maximum of 3 from either section)

Functions of wakes and fairs:

- In thanksgiving for harvest/end of harvest.
- Hiring fairs/mop fairs for finding employment.
- Social/bringing community together.
- Patronal festival of village church/saint's day.
- For lord of the manor to provide for his serfs.
- Courtship/meeting a mate.

Types of activities:

- Baiting sports/blood sports.
- Mob games single sticks/backswording.
- Races/smock races/races for prizes/wrestling/sack races.
- Folk sports/whistling matches/jingling matches/gurning or grinning contests/catching greasy pig/climbing greasy pole.
- Feasting/drinking/wagering.
- Courtship/sexual licence/promiscuity.

3   4 marks

4 marks for four from:

- Footmen employed as messengers/competitive runners/occupation became sport.
- Prize money for competitors/fame/status/money for food.
- A festival occasion/popular spectacle/exciting contest.
- Example of pedestrian: Robert Barclay Allardice walked 1000 miles in 1000 hours/Deerfoot the Native American visited England in 1860s.
- Wagering widespread.

4   4 marks

4 marks for four from:

- 'Boy culture'/organised by and for the boys/no master involvement.
- Institutionalised popular recreation/occasional.
- Low levels of organisation/no leagues/no cups/no competitions/no fixtures/no special kit/no special equipment.
- Low levels of skilfulness/no coaching/no coaches/often violent/often brutal/emphasis on force not skill.
- Using the natural environment; for example, rivers/fields/no specific facilities/no set pitches/no purpose-built courts.
- Some childlike games and pastimes; for example, running, spinning tops, playing with hoops.
- Activities adapted from home; for example, hare-and-hounds, mob football, cricket.

5   (a) 1 mark

1 mark for one from:

- Cricket has a code/rules which go beyond the end of the game and are a way of life.

(b) 1 mark

1 mark for one from:

- Character-building qualities more easily established through team games.
- Hare-and-hounds and fives did not require the courage or physicality of rugby or football.
- Hare-and-hounds and fives did not require the teamwork/co-operation of large team games.

- Hare-and-hounds and fives did not give opportunities of leadership/captaincy.
- Inter-school tennis fixtures for minor games did not rival those of major team games.
- Societal status of professional cricket and football higher than that of amateur status of athletics and fives.

(c) 1 mark

1 mark for one from:
- Tom Brown as the school cricket captain responsible for the team.
- Arthur/young boy sitting, has been looked after by Tom/regarded Tom as his role model/hero.
- Young master is a liberal young assistant master giving advice/very interested in reform/questions Tom's judgement/mutual respect.

6 3 marks

3 marks for three from:
- By teaching back in own school/next generation influenced.
- Through family/upbringing of own children.
- As community leaders.
- As industrial leaders/keen to give sport to their workers.
- As army officers/in the colonial service.
- As parsons/vicars/social Christians/needs of parishioners met.
- By forming sports clubs/national governing bodies.

7 6 marks

6 marks for six from:
First half of the century:

- Migration of lower classes from rural to urban areas/search for regular work/encouraged into urban areas.
- Loss of space.
- Shift from seasonal time to machine time/more structured lifestyle.
- Loss of time/12-hour days/no time to play.
- Poverty/low wages/working class as slaves to the factory in 1830s/no money to play.
- Poor working conditions/pollution.
- Poor living conditions/cramped/lack of health and hygiene provision/disease /no energy to play.
- Loss of rights/could not take part in previous activities; for example, mob football, blood sports/increased law and order/effective police force by mid-century.

Second half of the century:

- Provision of public baths in second half of century for cleanliness, and, later, for recreation; for example, swimming galas for middle class.
- Factory Acts improved conditions/opportunities for sport.
- 1870–90: Saturday half day – influence on spectatorism.
- The emergence of the new middle class in positions of authority.
- New middle-class attitudes/new ways of behaving and playing/the civilising process/old ways of playing changed.
- The influence of ex-public schoolboys in industry/the Church/local government/new ways of and reasons for taking part.
- Values of athleticism being spread to lower classes.
- Industrial patronage/provision for sport by wealthy industrialists; for example, provision of public parks for recreation in late nineteenth century.
- Excursion trips provided by some factory owners/trips to the seaside.
- Increased involvement of Church/acceptance and encouragement of sports and games by Church/Sunday school teams.

8 5 marks

5 marks for five from:

- Limited space to play traditional mob games/too far to go to countryside.
- Mob games no longer acceptable.
- Spectator provision/grandstands/terraces/football grounds.
- • Increased time/reduction of working week/Saturday half day/early closing movement.
- Workers had enough disposable income for gate money/cash to spend on Saturday.
- Regularity/improved rail network lead to regular fixtures.
- Improved transport/speed of travel/able to get to away matches.
- Bad working conditions made professional football a good job/a chance to escape from urban deprivation.
- Broken time payments/working class could not afford to miss work (and wages) to play – some became full-time professionals.

9 9 marks

9 marks for nine from:
(maximum of 3 for each syllabus – 1 from objective, 1 from content, 1 from method)

	1902 Model course	1933 syllabus	1950s (Moving and Growing/Planning the Programme)
Objectives	• Fitness for military service • Training in handling weapons • Discipline	• Physical fitness • Therapeutic results/health • Good physique • Good posture	• Development of physical/social/cognitive skills • Variety of experiences

	1902 Model course	1933 syllabus	1950s (Moving and Growing/Planning the Programme)
		• Development of mind and body/holistic aims	• Enjoyment • Personal satisfaction/ development • Involvement of all
Content	• Military drill/marching exercises • Weapons training • Deep breathing	• Athletics/gymnastic/ games skills • Group work	• Gymnastics/dance/ games skills/ swimming • Movement to music • Agility exercises • Apparatus work
Methodology	• Command style (e.g. 'attention') • In ranks • Group response/no individuality	• Mainly direct style/ centralised/some decentralised parts • Outdoor recommended • Some gymnasia	• Child-centred/ discovery/exploration/ individual interpretation of tasks • Problem solving • Enjoyment orientated • Progressive

Chapter 2 **Comparative studies**

1 **4 marks**

2 marks for two from: describing how a crisis has emerged in US PE.
Crisis:

* States are abolishing compulsory daily PE.
* Less need for fitness because military conscription has ended.
* Reducing PE saves money.
* Many school board members have a negative perception of PE.
* Child obesity is a growing concern.

2 marks for two from: explaining how the crisis is being addressed.
Addressing the crisis:

* Financial investment.
* Physical Education for Progress (PEP) programme.
* Strategies to develop curriculum.
* Strategies to train teachers.
* PE has been endorsed as the cornerstone of health by the NASPE.

2 **7 marks**

4 marks for four from: relating to the short-term benefits.
Short-term benefits:

* Attractive lifestyle at college.
* Opportunity to play at the higher levels.
* Self-esteem is dependent on athletic prowess.

- Single minded in their approach/acceptance of tough-minded approach/pragmatic role acceptance.
- Pro-draft possibilities.
- Most athletes know of no other lifestyle.

3 marks for three from: making points which relate to wider cultural attractions.
Wider cultural attractions:

- Progression towards the 'American Dream'/rags to riches.
- Opportunity to succeed and have financial security.
- Chance to be a winner.
- Opportunity to live out the Lombardian ethos.
- Chance to display manliness/frontierism.

3 4 marks

Four marks for four from:
Government policy/plan.

- Improved teacher training, for example more selective/CAPEPS.
- PE perceived as having cognitive/social importance.
- PE now has a contribution to make in holistic development/intellectual input.
- Links with military have been severed.
- Clear pathway from primary (five 'families' of activity) to Baccalaureate.
- Greatly reduced credibility gap.
- Increasing numbers who participate through to adulthood.

4 13 knowledge marks

13 marks are available for subject-specific knowledge.
(See Chapter 6 for further information about the synoptic question.)
(a) *7 marks maximum from:*

- Government policy; for example, de Gaulle's economic plan/investment by government in sport.
- Extend the base of the participation pyramid by increasing the opportunity for active involvement.
- Build multi-sports facilities in every major settlement.
- Maximise facility usage by implementing a national policy of joint provision.
- Improved PE and sport provision in schools.
- Establish policy *Sport pour Tous*/sport accessible to all.
- Sport promotes noble lifestyle.
- Sport desirable to good lifestyle.
- Ministry for Youth and Sport fund facilities at grass roots level.
- Funding from lottery.
- The club is the basic unit for sport in France and has policies for development and recruiting.
- Four federations promote sport; for example, Olympic federations, non-Olympic federations, associated federations and school and university federations.

- New sports; for example, golf is encouraged to expand.
- Sport is perceived to contribute to the health of the nation, education, culture and social life.

(b) 7 *marks maximum from:*

- Sport England's previous motto: More people, more places, more medals.
- Active Community Development Fund targets people under-represented in sport; for example, ethnic communities.
- Sport Action Zones target social and economically deprived areas.
- The Active Sports programme gets lottery funding for nine targeted sports; for example, athletics and basketball.
- The School Sport Co-ordinator programme aims to increase sports opportunities for young people.
- Governing bodies; for example, UK Athletics, encourage participation at all levels/organise local competitions/plan support programmes for clubs.
- Women's Sports Foundation promotes benefits of active lifestyles/initiates policy changes to increase opportunity.
- Disability Sport England encourages disabled people to play an active role in the development of their sports.
- Sports Coach UK has developed a coaching award structure.
- Sports Match gives £1 for every £1 given by business sponsorship to improve sports facilities at grass roots level.

5 5 marks

3 *marks for three from: answers that outline the problems.*
Problems:

- Spectator and player violence associated with ethnic rivalry.
- Refusal of the ethnics/new Australians to play the British/Colonial way.
- Soccer became a vehicle to express nationalistic sentiment; for example, Croatians and Macedonians.
- Soccer perceived as a game for the ethnics/soccer first branded a 'Pommie' game/discrimination by Anglo-Australians.
- Fear from Anglo-Australians that soccer would take over as the premier sport.
- Ethnic connection reduced media interest and sponsorship.

2 *marks for three from: points that identify how problems have been overcome.*
Overcoming problems:

- Banning ethnic team names, for example Sydney Croatia became Sydney United.
- Soccer officials have made efforts to de-ethnicise the game.
- Playing down/reducing the ethnic connection has increased positive publicity and brought in sponsors.
- Soccer official have rejected multi-cultural policy.
- Game increasingly used as a social unifier.

6 3 marks

1 mark for: explanation as to Aussie Rules being a new game

Aussie Rules football 'new game':

- Invented by Australians for Australia/was not an adopted game from the UK/'Motherland'.

2 marks for two from: describing why Australian Rules is a game for all people.

A game for all people:

- Social background – for players from every social background/for Aboriginals/Irish/English/Cornstalks.
- Social class – all levels of society watched.
- Frontierism – reflected frontier Australia/spirit of working together.
- National game – now adopted as the game of cosmopolitan Australia/spread beyond Victoria/now played in all states.
- Media – wide media appeal for all society.

7 4 marks

4 marks for four from:

- Affluence – population/can afford to engage in outdoor activities.
- Climate – favourable to outdoor lifestyle, for example beach culture.
- Frontierism – outdoor education experiences reflect frontier legacy of colonial times.
- Colonialism – influence of 'Motherland' and traditions of outdoor activities.
- Nationalism – pride in country.
- Urbanisation – a need to explore the outback/escapism.
- Demography – small population makes for expansive unpopulated areas.
- Landscape – genuine wilderness exists/uncharted territory with no population.
- Survival – necessary in a country with inhospitable climate and terrain.

Chapter 3 **Biomechanics**

1 (a) 4 marks

4 marks for:

- A–B: acceleration/increase in speed.
- B–C: constant speed.
- Newton 1: 'The ski jumper will move with constant velocity unless acted upon by an (unbalanced) force.'
- Explanation B–C: all forces cancel each other out/net force is zero.

(b) 4 marks

2 marks for:

- Air resistance/fluid friction.
- Friction (between skis and snow).

2 marks for two from:
(must have method and reason)

Method	Reason
Body (tuck) position	Reduce frontal/forward cross-sectional area
Body (tuck) position	More streamline/reduce drag behind skier/teardrop profile
Special clothing/lycra suits	Reduce surface friction effects between air and skier
Wax skis	Reduce friction between skis and snow

(c) 4 marks

3 marks for:
Generation:

- Ski jumper adopts aerofoil shape.
- Creates an angle of attack to the direction of airflow.
- Air travels further over the top of the ski jumper (or opposite).
- Therefore air travels faster over the top of the ski jumper (or opposite).
- Low pressure is created above ski jumper (or opposite).
- Bernoulli effect (lift force created).

1 mark for one from:
Effect:

- Extends the flight time/ski jumper travels further.
- Creates non parabolic/asymmetric flight path.

2 7 marks

(a) *1 mark for:*
- Longitudinal.

(b) *6 marks from:*
- Angular momentum of an object will remain constant unless an unbalanced/net angular force is placed upon it.
- Angular momentum = Iw/moment of inertia × angular velocity.
- Moment of Inertia of an object is its resistance to a change in angular motion.

Start of turn:

- Off centre/moment of force.
- Turn is initiated with a high MI/in crouched position/diagram C.
- Which gives a low angular velocity /some angular momentum.

During turn:

- MI is reduced/skier is more upright/diagram A.
- Therefore angular velocity/speed of turn is increased.

End of turn:

- MI is increased/skier returns to crouched position/diagram C.
- Angular velocity decreases.
- (Crouching stabilises skier at speed making it more difficult to turn.)

3 (a) 3 marks

3 marks for:
Weight and moment of force:

- Weight = 1000N
- Moment of force = force × (perpendicular) distance from the fulcrum/1000 × 0.2.
- Moment of force = 200Nm

(b) 4 marks

2 marks:
Force calculation:

- (principle of moments) clockwise moments = anticlockwise moments/ 0.25F = 200/F = $\frac{200}{0.25}$
- F = 800N (*units must be correct*)

2 marks two from:
Ankle as a lever system:

- Ankle is a class two lever system.
- Load/weight is closer to the fulcrum than effort/force of muscle contraction.
- Therefore, less effort is required to shift the equivalent load.

(c) 7 marks

5 marks from:
Newton's Laws of Motion to explain take off:

- Newton 1: 'An object will remain stationary unless an external/net/ resultant force acts upon it.'
- For the basketball player to leave the ground: the reaction force upwards must be greater than the weight of the basketball player/R > W.
- Newton 2: 'The acceleration of an object is directly proportional to the (net) force applied to it (and takes place in the same direction as the net force).'
- The basketball player accelerates (upwards).
- Newton 3: 'For every action there is an equal and opposite reaction.'
- The basketball player pushes downwards to the ground and the ground applies an equal and opposite force upwards on the basketball player.

2 marks from:

Vertical acceleration at take off:

- $F = Ma/a = \dfrac{F}{M} /a = \dfrac{R-W}{M}$

- $a = \dfrac{1500-1000}{100} /a = \dfrac{500}{100}$

- $a = 5ms^{-2}$ (units must be correct)

4 7 marks

7 marks (minimum one from each of three sections):

Centre of mass:

- Centre of mass is the point at which a body is balanced (in all directions)/point at which weight appears to act/the point in the body where all the mass appears to be concentrated.
- Position depends on the distribution of mass of the body/position can be varied by changing the shape of a body.

Take off:

- High position of CM/CM is raised by raising knee/raising both arms at take off.
- Reaction force passes through CM to prevent rotation during flight.

During flight

- CM follows predetermined (parabolic) flight path/height that CM reaches is predetermined at take off.
- Therefore basketball player lower CM/drops CM.
- By lowering high knee/dropping one arm.
- Therefore basketball player can reach higher.

Chapter 4 **Sport psychology**

1 4 marks

4 marks maximum, 2 for two from:
Type A characteristics:

- Highly competitive.
- Strong desire to succeed.
- Works fast.
- Likes to control.
- Prone to suffer stress.

4 marks maximum, 2 for two from:
Type B characteristics:

- Non-competitive.
- Unambitious.
- Works more slowly.
- Does not enjoy control.
- Less prone to stress.

2 4 marks

(Refer to either extrovert or introvert, not both)
Introvert:

2 marks maximum for two from:
- Nervous/shy.
- A loner.
- Less confident/anxious.
- Sensitive RAS.

2 marks maximum for two from:
Coaching implications:

- Lower arousal.
- Functions best at lower optimal.
- Imagery to eliminate the crowd.
- Raise self-efficacy.
- Positively reinforce performance.
- Environment must evoke calmness.

Extrovert:

2 marks maximum for two from:
- Relaxed/at ease.
- Gregarious.
- Confident/less anxious.
- Desensitised RAS.

2 marks maximum for two from:
Coaching implications:

- Increase arousal.
- Functions best at higher optimal.
- Performance is optimised in the presence of others.
- Will respond to negative reinforcement.
- Environment must evoke excitement.

3 4 marks

3 marks for:
Explanation of the triadic model:

- Cognitive component = knowledge of attitude object.
- Affective component = feelings toward the attitude component/evaluation.
- Behavioural component = response to the attitude object.

1 mark for:

Using model to change attitude:

- Dissonance theory: changing one component causes conflict/dissonance within the individual holding the attitude; for example, a negative attitude towards fitness could be modified if the knowledge component is changed, as in 'I don't like fitness training but it will improve my health.'

4   4 marks

3 marks for three from:
- Belief that failure is inevitable/no control over negative events.
- Linked to low achievers/avoidance behaviours/TAF personality characteristics.
- Past experiences negative.
- Specific learned helplessness associated with one skill.
- Global learned helplessness linked to all sports.
- Performer attributes failure to internal, uncontrollable and stable factors.
- Motivation is low.

1 mark for practical, for example:
- Declining to take part in racquet sports because of failure in badminton.

5   3 marks

3 marks for three from:
- Team performers will experience motivational problems during the course of a game. This may cause an individual to 'coast'/'social loafing'.
- Team co-ordination during play can prevent group potential being achieved.
- The greater the number of players, the more difficult it is to sustain team co-ordination or game plan/the Ringlemann effect.
- There is a link between social loafing and the Ringlemann effect; for example, the demotivated individual will relax effort, which in turn detracts from the team strategy.

6   2 marks

2 marks for:
- Task orientated – focus on group performance/meeting objectives/achieving goals.
- Social/person orientated – focus on good inter-personal relationships.

7   4 marks

4 marks for four from:
- Relations between leader and group are good/positive.
- Task is specific and clear.
- Leader has strong position of power/authority/respect.
- Leader has respect for the group.
- Team is highly motivated.
- Working environment is appropriate.
- Club/school/parents are supportive.

8   4 marks

4 marks for:

- External – narrow focusing on one external cue; for example, the ball in tennis serve.
- Narrow – internal inner focus/mental rehearsal on a specific cue; for example, concentration before the gun on a quick start in a sprint race.
- Broad – internal calculating a strategy through internal thought, but attention given to a wide range of options; for example, the coach working out a team plan.
- Broad – external attending to several cues from a changing environmental display; for example, a footballer making a pass.

9   3 marks

3 marks for 4 of:

- State confidence/confidence in a specific situation/self efficacy; for example, taking a penalty.
- Trait confidence/global confidence increases as state sport confidence increases; for example, penalty is successful.
- Mastery of skill/past experiences; for example, penalties have been scored previously.
- Styling/demonstration of skill level to others; for example, showing others the best way to take penalty.
- Vicarious experiences/watching others; for example, copying the best penalty-taker.
- Social support/verbal persuasion from team members; for example, assurance from colleagues that the penalty-taker has the skill to score.
- Effective leadership; for example, captain chooses penalty taker.
- Environmental comfort; for example, player is contented in the conditions.
- Situation favourableness – all environmental factors support the penalty taker.
- Physical/mental preparation will produce a better skill.
- Self-perception; for example, the penalty-taker is aware of strengths and weaknesses.

10 4 marks

4 marks for four from:

- Develop confidence/self efficacy.
- Set realistic/achievable goals.
- Focus on process goals (not outcome goals).
- Create opportunities for success.
- Positively reinforce success.
- Use attribution retraining.
- Attribute success to internal factors.
- Develop high Nach/approach behaviours/TAS personality characteristics.

11 **4 marks**

4 marks for four from:

- Playing in front of large crowds increases arousal levels/an increase in arousal will either facilitate or inhibit performance.
- Drive theory of social facilitation – increased arousal increases the likelihood of the dominant behaviour occurring.
- This will cause a deterioration of performance in weaker players because the dominant habit is likely to be incorrect.
- According to the inverted U hypothesis, optimal arousal levels differ according to personality type/extrovert personalities function best in conditions of high arousal due to a weak reticular activation system (RAS)/introverted personality types perform best at a lower point of arousal.
- Homefield advantage theory states that away teams are disadvantaged when faced by the home crowd.
- Proximity theory predicts that the closer the crowd is to the play, the higher the arousal level of the performers.
- Evaluation apprehension predicts the athlete is likely to experience increased arousal if the crowd is perceived to be knowledgeable and therefore passing judgement on the play.
- Distraction conflict theory predicts that a crowd will attract the attention of the player causing the possibility of information overload.

Unit 5 **Exercise Physiology**

Chapter 5 **Exercise and sport physiology**

1 **3 marks**

3 marks for:

A Phosphofructokinase/PFK/Glycogenphosphorylase/GPP.

B Sarcoplasm/cytoplasm.

C Sarcoplasm/mitochondria.

2 **3 marks**

1 mark for naming system:

- The lactic acid system/anaerobic glycolysis.

2 marks for two from:

- PC stores have been depleted.
- Glycogen/glucose is being broken down to pyruvic acid.
- Using the enzyme phosphofructokinase/PFK.
- Lactic acid is produced as a by-product.
- 2 ATP molecules are being regenerated.
- Insufficient/no oxygen.

3   3 marks

3 marks for three from:

- Reduce oxygen deficit/try and avoid OBLA/anaerobic threshold by controlling intensity.
- Warm up thoroughly before activity/improve oxygen supply, etc.
- 100 per cent replenishment of ATP/PC stores only takes 2–3 minutes.
- 50 per cent replenishment of ATP/PC stores only takes about 30 seconds.
- Rest intervals during training.
- Lactic acid removal is better with active sub-maximal warm down/therefore jog back to position/jog during stoppage time.
- As a coach, make sure you use all time outs/time for change of ends etc. to the full substitutions.
- Tactics employed, change to less demanding tactics to give rest.
- Anaerobic training improves body's ability to recover quicker.

4   6 marks

You must explain each principle and apply it to a named activity.

Maximum of 3 marks	Maximum of 3 marks
Specificity Training should be relevant to the individual and the sport for which they are training	• Energy systems used/fitness component • Muscle groups used/muscle fibre types recruited/type of muscular contraction used • Relevant movement patterns/neural pathways/skills
Progression Overload should be progressive. As the body adapts to the training demands, then further increases must follow to stimulate further improvement	Progression should be gradual
Overload Training should make the body work harder than usual. The body will then adapt and respond to this new level and fitness will be improved	• Increasing frequency of training • Increasing intensity of training • Increasing the time for training/duration
Reversibility If training reduces or stops, performance will deteriorate/physiological benefits are lost quickly/aerobic efficiency decreases faster than anaerobic efficiency	During holidays/breaks/injury, try and maintain fitness/use cross-training, e.g. swimming not running
Variance Training should include a variety of training types	• Maintain motivation and interest • Avoid overuse injuries • Give the body sufficient time to recover to avoid chronic exhaustion

Maximum of 3 marks	Maximum of 3 marks
Moderation Progressive overload should not be too sudden. This could lead to overtraining and injury to the muscular and/or skeletal systems	
Periodisation • Helps to ensure that optimal physiological and psychological peaks can be reached at the correct time for important competitions • Splits training into specific building blocks, each with its own specific goal.	Macro-cycle = long-term training block: 1–4 years Meso-cycles = intermediate training block: 1–4 months Micro-cycle = short-term training block: 1–3 weeks

5   **4 marks**

2 marks for:

Aerobic capacity.

Definition:

• The maximum amount of oxygen that can be taken in and used by the body (in one minute)/maximum capacity for oxygen consumption by the body/max VO_2/VO_2 max/maximal oxygen uptake.

Test:

• Treadmill test to exhaustion/Cooper's 12-minute run/NCF multistage fitness test (*not* bleep test)/Queen's College/Fitech/Harvard/Chester step test/PWC 170.

2 marks for:

Maximal strength.

Definition:

• The maximum force that can be generated by a muscle in a single contraction.

Test:

• There are numerous tests that are specific to local muscular regions as well as whole body exercise. Make it clear that test must be 1 RM/ONE REPETITION MAXIMUM, for example hand grip dynamometer/grip test/leg dynamometer/snatch/bench press/standing broad jump/sergeant jump/vertical jump or equivalent.

6   5 marks

5 marks for five from:

Vascular system:

Due to aerobic training, the triathlete has:

- better oxygen-carrying capacity in the blood/more oxygen transported
- (due to) increased number of red blood cells/more haemoglobin
- decrease in blood viscosity/enhanced ease of blood flow
- (due to) an increase in blood plasma/the water component of the blood
- enhanced vascular shunt mechanism
- (due to) improved elasticity/stronger arteriole/artery walls
- improved gaseous exchange at the alveolar–capillary membrane
- (due to) capillarisation on the alveoli wall/lungs
- improved gaseous exchange at the tissue–capillary membrane
- (due to) capillarisation in the muscle (cell)
- increased tolerance to lactic acid
- (due to) an increased efficiency of the blood buffering system
- raised anaerobic threshold
- (due to) improved removal of lactic acid.

Note: 1 mark only for capillarisation, 1 mark only for gaseous exchange.

7 4 marks

4 marks for four from:
- Static stretching/active.
- Athlete moves into a position that takes the joint just beyond its point of resistance.
- Passive stretching.
- Partner moves athlete into a position that takes the joint just beyond its point of resistance.
- Soft tissue around joint is lengthened.
- Position held for minimum of six seconds.
- Ballistic stretching/dynamic.
- Athlete uses momentum to move a body part through its extreme range of movements; for example, using swinging leg/arm movements.
- Ballistic stretching should only be done by athletes who are already flexible.
- PNF (proprioceptive neuromuscular facilitation) stretching.
- The muscle undergoes an isometric contraction then muscle is relaxed.
- Seeks to inhibit the stretch reflex mechanism.
- So that a greater stretch can be performed next time.
- Stretches should be repeated during session.
- For maximum benefit at least three times a week.
- Better performed when muscles are warm/during warm up/cool down.

8 4 marks

2 marks for definition, 2 marks for tests:

Component	Definition	Test
Agility	The ability to change direction/body position at speed/the combination of speed and co-ordination	Illinois agility run/hexagonal obstacle text
Balance	The ability to maintain equilibrium/the centre of mass/gravity over the base of support	Time on a balance board/beam/stork stand test
Co-ordination	The ability to put the relevant motor programmes in the right order/to effectively use the neuromuscular system to produce smooth/efficient movement/the interaction of the motor and nervous systems	Alternate hand wall toss test/time taken to learn how to juggle/hexagonal obstacle text
Reaction time	The time between detection of a stimulus and the initiation of the response	The ruler drop test/pushing a button in response to a light coming on

Component	Definition	Test
Speed	The maximum rate that a person can move over a specific distance/the ability to put body parts into motion quickly	<100m sprint

9 4 marks

4 marks in total:

Answers include (Recombinant) erythropoietin, (Rh)EPO, blood doping, human growth hormone, HGH, amphetamines, *not* beta blockers, anabolic steroids, masking agents, diuretics, *or* any legal ergogenic aid, for example physiological aids such as altitude training; nutritional aids such as creatine, glutamine, carbohydrate loading; or mechanical aids such as nasal strips.

EPO/Blood doping

Benefits:

- Stimulates red blood cell production/more red blood cells.
- Increases the blood's oxygen-carrying capacity/allows more oxygen to be delivered to tissues.
- Increases haemoglobin.
- Increases VO_2 max/endurance.

Negative effects:

- (Rh)EPO or blood doping reduces heart rate/increases heart rate.
- Increases blood viscosity/blood pressure.
- Increases risk of blood clotting/heart failure.
- Reduces natural production of EPO/erythropoietin.

- (if blood is received from a donor) reinfused blood could be mismatched triggering an allergic reaction/athletes could contract hepatitis/AIDS/any blood-carried disease.
- Athletes can experience chills/fever/nausea.

Human growth hormone (HGH)

Benefits:

- Human growth hormone stimulates protein/nucleic acid synthesis in skeletal muscle/aids muscle growth/increases muscle mass.
- Human growth hormone stimulates bone growth (important for young athletes).
- Human growth hormone gives overall decrease in body fat.
- Human growth hormone increases blood glucose levels.
- Human growth hormone enhances healing after musculoskeletal injuries.

Negative effects:

- Human growth hormone increases possibility of abnormal growth/ acromegaly/bone thickening which causes broadening of hands/feet/face/skin thickening.
- Human growth hormone causes enlargement of internal organs/soft tissue growth.
- Human growth hormone causes muscle/joint weakness.
- Human growth hormone causes heart disease.
- Human growth hormone causes glucose intolerance/diabetes/hypertension/high blood pressure.

Amphetamines

Benefits:

- Amphetamines stimulate central nervous system/CNS.
- Amphetamines increase redistribution of blood flow to skeletal muscles.
- Amphetamines elevate free fatty acids.
- Amphetamines increase muscle tension.

Negative effects:

- Amphetamines (due to delaying the onset of fatigue) enable athletes to push dangerously beyond normal limits to the point of circulatory failure/mask injury.

10 4 marks

1 mark for definition:

- A form of diet aimed at increasing the amount of glycogen stored in the muscles/liver.

2 marks for two from:
- Deplete/empty stores of glycogen through training.
- Have high protein/fat diet (for 2–3 days)/low-carbohydrate diet.
- Three days on high carbohydrate diet prior to the event.

1 mark for benefits:
- Carbo-loading benefits endurance athletes as it helps to offset fatigue/they can work for longer/anaerobic athletes who have to compete many times in a short space of time.